FIFTY SUMMERS
IN CAPE BRETON

John Tyler Bonner

With a note on Cape Breton music
by Jonathan Bonner

FOREWORD

We have been spending the summers in Cape Breton Island for fifty years. Right from the beginning we knew we had found the right place. On these pages I want to give my version of the essence of Cape Breton and the Margaree River valley and what they have meant to me and my family. I am a biologist and teach at Princeton University; this means I have the summers off and it is where I do my writing, this summer being no exception as these words attest.

At the end of last summer I had a visit from my friend Mary K MacLeod who is a professor of history at Cape Breton University and who comes originally from St. Rose, just a few miles from where we live now. She has written a number of books on different aspects of Cape Breton's history. We were talking about how things were in the old days, and after telling some anecdotes (which are in this book) she urged me to write something about how the Margaree River Valley and the rest of Cape Breton had changed over the fifty of our summers here. And she urged me to include the anecdotes. The idea took in my mind and the pages that follow are the result. The reader must be prepared for an ambling, very personal account of my recollections and perceptions. I am not a historian and this is in no sense a history. It is a stirring up of the contents of the attic that is my brain, and I can only hope the recollections are close to reality.

A number of people have read it, and straightened me out on many points to make what I say closer to the truth, and I am very grateful for their help. In particular I want to thank my children (who are no longer children!), Rebecca, Jonathan, Jeremy and Andrew for their help filling in the gaps with their own recollections. And in this I include my niece Hannah who lives in Mallorca, Spain and has visited us on numerous summers. And her father, my brother Tony, also from Mallorca, who came one summer and had some most helpful suggestions. I thank my friend Slawa Lamont–who lives in Margaree–and helped me in many ways. Special thanks to George Thomas for allowing me to use five of his photographs from his splendid book, *Photographs of Cape Breton,* and to my friend the artist, Angela Grauerholz for transferring them to my book, and to my colleague Henry Horn who kindly rescued my old kodachromes for the other figures.

And Frank MacDonald the author and newspaper man was kind enough to check the ms. for facts and told me some splendid anecdotes of his own. Heartfelt thanks also to my son Jonathan, the artist, who designed the cover. It shows my granddaughter Ondine and myself looking towards the future of Cape Breton. Finally my particular thanks to Robert Morgan, who is not only a real historian, but THE historian of Cape Breton. He had so many good suggestions on an early draft, that if there is any merit in these pages, it is probably his fault!

CHAPTER 1

For me the summer is the time for writing: to escape from the bustle of academic life and have the peace and time for some uninterrupted thoughts. In 1947 my first job after the second world war was to teach biology at Princeton University where I have been ever since. It has been the perfect place for me, but I found it almost impossible to write anything that required continuity during the school year. Fortunately there were no classes over the summer so I could escape and leave the laboratory for few months and write. Those books that were created in Cape Breton were not light-hearted novels, but weighty arguments on some basic principles of biology. As far as I was concerned it was the perfect life: research and teaching which I loved for the school year, and writing during the summer which I loved with equal enthusiasm.

We had spent a few previous summers on the Maine coast, but for various reasons that became unsatisfactory, and thanks to a recommendation from a friend in the music department at Princeton, we looked into a cabin they had rented in the Margaree river valley that might be available. The idea was very attractive, with the result that in June of 1959 my wife Ruth, the children, Jonathan aged 12, Jeremy 8, Andrew 4, and Phoebe the much loved basset hound, all piled into our station wagon and drove the 1100 miles to the Margaree. Our daughter, Rebecca 15, stayed back home with friends.

If one glances at a map one can see that our route was essentially east. People in Maine say they are located "down east" and Cape Bretoners will also use the word "down" to indicate going in a northeast direction. So we were going down to the Margaree River valley. Our road took us up the coast, through Providence, Rhode Island, around Boston and along the edge of Maine to Calais where we went through Canadian customs and crossed into New Brunswick. It was a very different trip than it is today and took considerably longer. The reason is that all sorts of super highways have appeared that were not there then. In New Brunswick we would weave through the country roads among the farms. The biggest difference is that now there are modern roads that go around the cities; we used to have to struggle with going right through town in St. John and Moncton, which was not only slow, but we were in constant danger of getting lost. Even the unfamiliar traffic lights were a new challenge.

In one of those early years we had two major disappointments on the trip, both connected to the tides. I do not know exactly what we expected of the reversing falls in St Johns, but all there was to see is the water pouring through by a bridge; and it was either going in one direction or the other. To get the full effect one would have to stare at it for many hours, and we were just passing through. The other was the tidal bore at Moncton. Somehow we imagined a great wall of water racing up the river with the rising tide at the speed of a galloping horse, but what we saw was a pathetic ripple, more like the speed of a galloping mouse. That ripple did indeed move up river, but our dreams were shattered.

We entered Nova Scotia through the wind swept Tantramar marshes and from Amherst took the northern costal road through Pugwash and River John; a lovely drive. Then through—not around!—two big towns, New Glasgow and Antigonish. I no longer remember where we spent the last night, but it was mid morning when we began descending a long slope, and there before us was Cape Breton spread across the other side of a narrow band of ocean, less than a mile across. This is the Canso Straight that makes Cape Breton an island. It was a beautiful sunny day and the sight was glorious; the water glittered in the sun and the rounded hills beyond were green and solid. It matched the excitement we all felt.

We did not realize then that the stone causeway across to the island had only been completed in 1955, four years earlier. Until then a ferry was the only way to get across. Even train cars were rolled onto a barge and hooked up at the other end. Apparently the Straight of Canso had been a regular migration route for tuna, and after the causeway, which is a submerged pile of rocks torn from an adjacent mountain, blocked their passage. I was told that if one was there at the right time one could see the gigantic, frustrated fish leaping right out of the water close to the road. By the time we got there they had found a new route.

At the end of the causeway there is a lock to allow boats to cross the divide because the ocean level on both sides can vary with the tides. One year the drawbridge was up (or rather rotated 90 degrees so the boats could pass) and a submarine was going through the lock. What joy for our young children. We poured out of the car and watched the submarine come to the right level, with our young having a brisk conversation with the sailors. Other times I have been blocked there due to a passing boat and they were more frustrating and a test of my patience.

Nothing seemed so beautiful as we motored along the slanting coast past Craignish looking out onto the ocean. The next place that arrested us was Mabou and its surroundings. A whole series of spruce covered hills and picturesque farms here and there. I still remember parking the car on the side of the road, getting out, and just taking it all in: the blue sky, the few puffy clouds, and the brisk, pure air. Inverness, a mining town looked bleaker, but more on that later.

We finally arrived at lunchtime in Margaree Forks and stopped to eat at the Margaree Lodge (then run by Dr. and Mrs. MacIsaac) and found a table by the big window which gave us an incredible view. The South West and the North East branches off the Margaree meet at the Forks and we could see the junction and the main river as it flowed away from us north to the ocean. The valley lies between two rows of hills covered with spruce and it was green and fertile with farms below; a sight that lifted our hearts.

Let me now say some general things about Cape Breton. It is an island at the northern end of Nova Scotia in Canada and roughly the same size as the big island of Hawaii, but larger than the island of Mallorca–part of Spain in the Mediterranean– where my brother and his family have lived for over fifty years. All three islands could not possibly be more different. In Hawaii there are great numbers of people (and automobiles!) enjoying the mild weather all year around with beautiful spots surrounded by great expanses of lava, and some of the housing developments are built right on these depressing, grey landscapes. Mallorca is also densely populated and equally invaded by masses of tourists, but they are concentrated around the edges near the beaches. Like Hawaii there are many beautiful spots; but it is very different, with picturesque villages, many old houses, from modest ones to the grand fincas of the old nobility. Unlike Hawaii, and like Cape Breton, Mallorca has four genuine seasons, although they are very much warmer than Cape Breton. The changes of the last fifty years in Mallorca have some similarities with those of Cape Breton.

In comparing these three islands, Cape Breton is indeed very different. For starters there are fewer people. The resident population amounts to a mere 104 thousand, and the summer residents, like my family, can be counted in the hundreds. The passing tourists mostly motor around the island in a few days and stop briefly at some of the more spectacular beauty spots, such as along the Cabot Trail that winds through the northern National Park. The road hugs the steep hills all covered with trees and the precipitous view of the ocean below is a wonder.

The people of Cape Breton hail from a number of separate heritages. The first inhabitants for thousands of years were the Mi'kmaq who are still very much there on their reservations in five locations on the island. They are a proud people who, in recent years, have regained much of their deserved respect.

Perhaps the largest influx came from Scotland some time ago, and a glance at the relatively small telephone book of the Island will reveal an amazing number of names beginning with "Mac". There are also a very large numbers who immigrated from Ireland, and in certain areas there is a significant French population. The Acadian French came very early in the history of the Island and were so infamously expelled by the British in 1758 after they conquered the magnificent fort at Louisbourg. Some removed to other areas, especially on Isle Madame in southern Cape Breton, but there was also a subsequent influx of Acadians from Prince Edward Island and St. Pierre et Miquelon—the latter being islands that still belong to France. Serious immigration from England began in 1768 and another wave in 1785 of loyalists who moved north from the new-founded United States.

Some of the local communities tend to be predominantly homogeneous. For instance the north side of the estuary of the Margaree river and up the coast are mostly Acadian French with villages named Belle Côte, Terre Noire, Cap Le Moine, St. Joseph du Moine, Grande Étang right to up the large town of Cheticamp. The other side of the river is primarily Scottish with names like St. Rose, Dunvegan, and Inverness. There is even a very small community on Scotch Hill. And the early English are represented by another small community called Smithville. The Irish are settled in a more diffuse fashion up river. I once asked Dr. Tompkins (a relative of Rose's; more about her in a moment) why there was another Tomkins family so far away up Big Brook, a tributary to the Margaree. He said that when his ancestors settled from the old country they thought it was safer to settle in two places quite removed from one another. He said they wanted be sure that there was a safe haven if some landlord came to evict them. They had brought along their scars from Ireland.

As I proceed I will have many things to say of these different peoples and how they fit—or do not fit—together. And also show how much it has changed in the last 50 years. And now more about our arrival.

After lunch at Margaree Forks we knew we had to drive down the east side of the river for our destination was Fordview. First we took the old Doyle's bridge (with the high iron frame above it—it has been replaced twice since then) over the North East Margaree branch of the river, and then on to a very narrow dirt road—no, it seemed more of a track than a road, with trees often leaning into it. Somewhat apprehensively we arrived at Ford-view and were greeted by Rose Tompkins at her large, old farmhouse with the cabin behind.

Rose Tompkins room and boarding house with the barn across the dirt road Our cabin on the left foreground. The Margaree river can be seen just beyond. The Post Office was in the small, one story protuberance on the left of the main house, and my study was just above it.

Rose made us feel welcome and we were soon settled in the cabin.

Our cabin at Fordview.

It had two small bedrooms, a minimal bathroom with a shower and a narrow kitchen with a good size wood range. It kept us warm on cool days and at night and roasted us on warm summer days. (I soon learned that one had to know what one was doing to boil water on a wood stove; we used our Coleman camp stove!) The water came through the stove in a coiled pipe: that was our hot water. All the water was from a little brook behind the cabin and it was always wonderfully clear, and cold! There was a narrow porch facing the Margaree river along one side, with the farm house to the right. We would sit there after dinner and watch the river, the hills beyond and all the glory in the slanting sun. There was a magic to it that never dimmed. And occasionally a bit of excitement like the time a sparrow hawk flew across close by us with a minute humming bird in hot pursuit. It was as though it was being chased by a hypodermic needle: the little one was besting the big one in no uncertain terms.

A couple of years later our Jeremy in Princeton found some baby wood duck on the road and brought them home. No one seemed to know how to feed and raise them, so to his intense sorrow we released them back in a marsh near where they were found. To buck up his spirits we bought him two practically new born mallard ducklings from a local farm and they came with us all the way to Cape Breton. (At each motel on the way up we would immediately put some water in the bath tub and they would cruise around in ecstasy.) They turned out to be two females: Matsey and Flatfoot. For obvious reasons they were never allowed into the cabin, but they would join us on the porch making low conversational warbling noises that Jeremy answered. He was the only one of us who could speak their language. Later in the summer, when they could fly, they would spot us as we walked down to the river to swim, swoop down and land beside us, and walk (waddle) behind us the rest of the way. When we got to the water's edge they would not go into the water until we did, and they would come out the moment we emerged. They had a grand time swimming in and around us. At the end of the summer one was killed by an owl or a fox, and the other flew off, we hoped to find other friends.

I needed a place to write and was able to rent a small room in the old farm house (now a room and boarding house) that looked over the apple orchard and unfortunately the cabin. Unfortunate because I could see the children playing and occasionally had to lean out of the window and yell something like, "Jonathan, get down off that tree." But every morning I managed to scrawl out my daily quota of words that I imposed on myself, and then lunch and an afternoon out of doors.

Our landlady Rose Tompkins (who was also the Fordview postmistress) was exceedingly good and helpful to us right from the beginning. She was short and built sturdy and square, and was a person of an admirably strong character: we immediately became her subjects. It just so happened my dear wife, Ruth, had an equally strong character, so it was not long before they locked horns. As so often happen they very quickly decided the other was their kind of person and soon got along famously. Ruth taught Rose how to make decent coffee—it should not look like weak tea—and Rose, who was a gifted cook, gave Ruth some splendid recipes. We decided we could afford two dinners a week at Rose's boarding house which we all loved. In her kitchen Rose had a huge range and all the cooking was done over a wood fire. She had innumerable nieces who were commandeered to help Aunt Rose with the chores, and like a good sergeant she kept them hopping. All the young called her Aunt Rose, even our own children.

She also had a friend, Sarah Delaney, a school teacher and a gentle soul, more or less her age, who came to help in the busy summer. There was a fenced-in vegetable patch which I could see from my desk in the big house, and one day the gate had been left open and a cow sauntered in. I rushed out as did Sarah to shoo the cow out. Sara picked up a stick and whacked the cow on the rump with the words, "Get out of here you son-of-a-bitch." I said, "Sarah, what sort of language is that from a person as dignified as you." She explained that she never used that kind of language with people, but it was quite OK to talk that way to cows. I had a lot to learn.

Our cabin was inside the edge of a rather large pasture. Mostly the cows avoided us, but in the middle of one night a cow started scratching her back on a corner of the cabin: there was a tremendous noise and the whole cabin shook and vibrated; we all thought the end of the world had come.

One other bit of country life that I have not seen these days. One day I was walking from the house to the cabin and Rose and Sarah were by the garden with a fire, a pile of wood ashes and a bucket of lard. They were making soap the old way.

CHAPTER 2

Farming was very different then than it is now. In the first place there were many more farms, and in the valley they were mostly dairy farms. Today what cattle are raised are mostly for beef. And there were very many more sheep then than there are now. In small part the difference can be accounted for by the sudden invasion of coyotes a few years after we came. Their eastward spread was evident everywhere, but how did they cross onto Cape Breton? I think it unlikely they came on the causeway; more likely they came across the ice in the frozen winter. In any event, as they became more numerous they were a serious threat to the sheep. Some farmers simply gave up, but others acquired European sheep-guarding dogs such as white maremmas, originally from Italy, and one farm by the lower river put a jackass with the flock. I remember this well for I was fishing in a place where there was a thin row of trees hiding the pasture close behind. Suddenly I heard the most incredibly loud rasping noise that nearly gave me a heart attack. After I calmed down I realized it was a vocal jackass tending its flock.

Rose's room and boarding house had two farms close by; Alec and Loretta Miller and their large family up a hill short ways, and Patrick and Catherine Tompkins and their large family right next door. Their children and ours soon became fast friends. Patrick's milk cows were in a barn and after milking he would set his big stainless steel cans by the road and they were picked up and taken to get Pasteurized and bottled. Rose took some of the cream and made her delicious butter. She used an old fashioned electric clothes washing machine where the central moving part was attached to a butter churning paddle—no more of that hand turning. I asked Patrick if I could get raw milk for the family which he immediately supplied. At first it was perfect, but suddenly one day it had a horrible taste: the cows were eating something different. When I told him that we had difficulty drinking it, he laughed and said they all drank it anyhow; it was just a matter of getting used to it.

Let me pause here to say something about Patrick and his family.

Patrick and Catherine Tompkins and their family. Their six children and a friend of theirs standing behind. Young Patrick is at the wheel of their new tractor. (Photograph by George Thomas.)

They were absolutely splendid people: to me they were the personification of an idealized Cape Breton family. There were other families who were similar, but the Tompkins are the ones I got to know best. Patrick himself was incredibly hard working, as was Catherine with all her house chores, her six children and all those hungry mouths to feed. Patrick's day started very early and never seemed to stop well into the evening. He did all the chores outside such as chopping wood, tending the garden, repairs on the house, and of course the cows that had to be milked twice a day. The MacDonald brothers, Charlie and Myles, had a very big dairy farm down the road near Doyle's Bridge and one very hot summer day our car became surrounded and trapped in the middle of their huge herd on the way to the barn to be milked. We slowed to about 2 miles per hour; just their speed. Charlie MacDonald, even redder than usual on that hot day, was walking beside our car and suddenly turned, with not a very happy face and said, "It's always cow time."

Perhaps one of the biggest differences between then and now is that horses have been replaced by tractors. This was a world-wide change and my brother reported that in Mallorca the farmer's mules were replaced in the same way. He told me that in the village they lived in—perhaps the size of Inverness—on a particular saint's day (I think it was for St. Francis of Assisi) everyone brought their mules to the courtyard of the lovely old 18th century church to have them blessed by the priest. Early in those transition years one of the farmers brought his tractor for the traditional blessing. Apparently the priest did bless it but announced firmly that from then on it was animals only. The mules have disappeared and pets have taken their place at the church ceremony.

One effect of the disappearance of horses in Cape Breton was the disappearance of blacksmiths. When we came there was only a few left: one was Lawrence Bennett whose forge was between the Forks and Northeast Margaree by the Brook pool.

William Bennett the blacksmith at his forge by the road at the Brook pool.

What was most noticeable when he had his fire going was the lack of a chimney. The smoke would pour out of the upper portion of his large doorway; it looked as though the whole building was about to go.

In the valley when we first arrived it was essentially horses only. I used to watch Patrick cut the hay on his mower: he and his horse seemed to work perfectly together. They even managed to go side-ways, tilted along a steep slope that looked pretty tricky to uneducated me. Then after a time to dry, he and his horse would rake it into rows, the rake consisting of a two-wheeled sulky-like vehicle with great curved teeth that could be raise or lowered to line the dry hay up in rows. There was a day, long gone, when the cutting was all done by a row of men with scythes and later raked with hand rakes. So already what I was seeing in 1960 was in itself a step towards modern efficiency. There is a tragic irony here: a few years ago Patrick was killed by his tractor which ran over him. It was a huge loss for us all.

Putting the hay in the hay wagon was entirely done by people with pitchforks.

The men loading the hay wagon with one of the children leading the horse.

It was slow and sweaty work in the hot summer days. When today I see a modern mower, and a rake, and then a bailer come sweeping though a field, doing everything in fast time, it is hard to remember what it used to be like. It is similar to the change from a crow quill pen to an up-to-date computer: the increase in efficiency is vast, but at the same time some desirable intangibles are lost.

The next step was putting the hay in the barn. After parking the wagon inside the barn door onto the threshing floor, the horse was unhitched and brought out to the barn yard where it was attached by a rope to the pitching machine that hung from a track above. The pitching machine was a steel spike about 3 feet long with a four inch tip that could be turned at right angles by pushing a lever at the top. This spike was pressed down into the hay load and the tip was then switched to its 90° position so that when it was pulled up a great bunch of hay came with it. The other end of the rope was attached to the horse who was then led away from the barn first lifting the gathered hay high in the air, and then rolled on the track along the ridge pole of the barn and dumped in the loft. The great thing about this maneuver was that the boys were allowed to lead the horse back and forth.

**Jonathan driving King to operate the
pitching machine in the barn.**

They took turns and never seemed to tire. They were also allowed to drive the horse pulling the hay wagon or the hay rake and other machines. Now the great machines do it all in a trice, (by one man) and there is no place for the eager youngsters.

Because there were pitchforks in the barn that could be hidden in the hay Alec Miller, who was overseeing the whole operation, got the children together and informed them sternly that absolutely no one was to jump on the hay, especially from the loft down to the hay which lay deep on the ground floor. But it was irresistible, and Alec caught Jonathan doing exactly that, and immediately put him over his knee and gave him a good spanking. It solved the problem instantaneously and Ruth and

I were delighted, mixed with some surprise. It was all part of the haying and raising children in those early days.

There was one big difference between the children's lives in Princeton compared to Cape Breton. In Princeton it was more-or-less the accepted rule that you played with kids your own age. When we came to Fordview there was a great span, from those in their early teen ages down to four year olds. The two older Miller girls, Ann and Mary were the bosses and they kept a careful eye on the toddlers and a stern control over those in between, but they all seemed to be having a wonderful time.

Some of the children of on a walk at East Margaree with the Miller family. From left to right, Jeremy, Lawrence Miller, Anne Miller, Andrew, Mary Miller, and Gerard Miller. (There is someone behind Anne who I cannot identify.)

They would wander about in a group, like a well tended flock, exploring everything such as the edge of the small brook, or playing games in the barn. Of course us adults never really knew what was going on; all we could see was they were very cheerful and our boys entered in as thought there had never been any other way to behave. For our young boys there was no better place to be than on a farm, from both their point of view and ours. I have a colleague, a fellow biologist at Princeton, who is wonderfully sensible and level headed. I asked her one day what made her that way and she said that she and her sister grew up on a farm in Wisconsin. There being no sons in the family every morning before school they had to milk the cows and bring in the eggs. Think what a better person I would be if I had had that kind of an upbringing!

When we first came to the valley we did most of our shopping at Bernie Doyle's store in Margaree Forks, or at Hastings Laurence's store in Margaree Harbour (we still do: happily his son Fletcher still carries on in his father's tradition).

Bernie Doyle in his store. (Photograph by George Thomas.)

Hastings Laurence in his store. (Photograph by George Thomas.)

All three are quite splendid people. Bernie was a courteous and rather shy man who was invariably helpful. Hastings was a severe looking person who always surprised me for despite his lordly appearance, he had a puckish sense of humor. He understood human folly and handled it with tolerance. One day I bought some vanilla extract that Ruth needed for cooking, and he mysteriously looked under the counter and came up with a bottle. In some surprise I asked why did he keep it hidden there, and with a wry smile he told me that it contained alcohol and some of his older male customers were a little bit over eager to get their hands on some. Another time I said that a new coffee pot that was for sale seemed rather expensive to me.

He said, "Oh yes, I just got that in for the summer millionaires."

Both stores had all the basic staples: sugar and all the other baking needs, and so forth, and a good variety of canned goods. Vegetables were rare, although during the summer they would have some things from local farms, such as utterly delicious strawberries.

It was difficult to find good beef, or as it was called, western beef. The only store that carried it was Ralph Macpherson's Lucky Dollar store way up river at Frizzleton (now Margaree Valley). One day someone had an old cow slaughtered and it was skinned and hung up from three teepee-like poles in the yard in front of Rose's house. All the neighbors came and bought a cut that was sliced off. We decided to try it too and bought some liver. It turned out to be a great mistake on our part: we learned why the liver we normally bought came from calves.

Laurence's General Store also sent out a small truck every day that went to all the farms in the neighborhood. This was the daily mission of Tommy Ben MacDonald. He was a small man with a huge heart whom we got to know well later as he was our next door neighbor when we moved to Margaree Harbour. He would park in Rose's yard, open the back doors and put out some steps. As the customer entered she was surrounded by shelves jammed full of the store's most popular items. It was a fantastic service to the housewives of the area, especially those, of which there were many, who did not have the use of a car. The store came to them. One of the results of these daily voyages was that Tommy Ben knew everyone, and everyone knew—and liked—Tommy Ben.

Another commercial enterprise that I remember vividly was the Lebanese peddler Melvin Taha who came door to door in the whole area. He came on foot carrying the most enormous load with his wares— a huge black cube carried over his shoulder with a leather strap. How he managed will always be a mystery to me. He was a cheerful person and when he came to Rose's we had a glimpse his rather remarkable stock, mostly of dry goods and samples of material that could be ordered. For some time he came annually from Lebanon and then later set up a small shop in Northeast Margaree. He has long gone along with many of the other things that were small and individualistic in the valley.

Last, but definitely not least, was Jim Smith's large two-story store in North East Margaree. So far as I remember he did not deal in food or medicine, but literally everything else. Household and kitchen wares, hardware, and only Jim knew what more, but it seemed to be without limit. As one entered the store everything was piled high on the tables and the floor separated by a narrow isle or two. I think of the stacks as higher than the standing height of a person, but that may be because it has grown in my mind over the years. One could do nothing without Jim, a rather heavy set man with a friendly face. He, and only he, knew where to find things. So shopping went something like this: "Jim, do you have a cheese grater?" He would pause with a fixed, concentrating stare for a bit, and then dash off to some distant pile, rummage around its base, and pop back into view with a triumphant smile holding a cheese grater. Alas, after Jim's death the store burnt down around 1970 and is no more. I always though that it went to join him.

I would now like to reminisce on a matter that is neither delicate nor romantic. The subject of garbage may seem like an inappropriate subject in a discussion of the last fifty years of Cape Breton, but there has been a big change. In our early years there was no garbage collecting. In Fordview we had to motor up the road towards Cheticamp to Cap Le Moine where there was a steep bank falling right in to the sea. It is a most beautiful spot: an incredible view up and down the coast and out across the ocean. There was a place to park the car off the road and one just threw everything down the cliff on top of an impressive pile of human detritus. Besides decaying food there were old broken refrigerators and every conceivable item of human refuse. If one lived inland sink holes near a back road were used in the same way. (Needless to say there was no such thing as recycling and paper was simply burned in an old, rusty metal barrel in one's back yard.) Today the old spot on the coast is pristine: nothing is left but the beauty. That is real progress.

Now a truck comes very early on Monday morning which not only takes the neatly bagged garbage, but even the objects to be recycled in a different color bag. I particularly appreciate the way the garbage man treats my big can. He puts the lid back on, and if it is windy, he puts the empty can in the ditch so it will not blow away. Back home in Princeton the garbage man just flings the can to one side, often right out into the road. Cape Breton clearly has a big edge over New Jersey.

Another change in the last fifty years can be seen in schooling. One room school houses, at least for the lower grades, were still common when we arrived. In fact there was one in Fordview taught by Loretta Miller, and there was another in Margaree Harbour. They were very simple houses that were more-or-less the size of the one room they contained. Today I think there is only one remaining as a school for the younger children in Pleasant Bay. To me the greatest paean to one room school houses appeared as a letter to the editor in the Oran, the weekly newspaper, just a few years ago. It talks about a school way up in the Big Intervale much earlier than 1959 but it says so much and with enviable charm:

Letter to the ORAN in the 14 October 1998 issue
Dear editor,

Several years ago I read an article in the Oran concerning a little church in Big Intervale.

Words cannot describe the memories that came back to me, Where has the time gone?

It all began in August, 1944. The war was still raging and so many of our young men and women were serving their country. Teachers were in demand to the point of emergency. Inspector Robertson decided to use newly graduated high school graduates to fill in as teachers. I received letter from Inspector Robertson asking if I would accept a teaching position in Big Intervale on what he referred to as a Permissive License. You could teach for only one year with this license, then attend Normal College. I accepted the position. I was green as a cabbage and nervous my leaving home on my own for the first time.

I arrived in Big Intervale and was fortunate enough to be taken in as a boarder with Mr. & Mrs. Dan Willie Murray. They owned a beautiful home which was sort of a bread and breakfast. Many men from around the province to fish salmon in the Margaree river and some men came to hunt deer. So, the Murrays catered to many people.

The school house was located about a mile away. Fourteen children attended. They were amazed to see me since their previous teachers were much older.

Big Intervale is located about eight (8) miles from Frizzleton, nestled between two mountains.

Margaree river winds its way through a valley. All the inhabitants there were of Scottish descendents and very traditional, kind, generous, hard working and loving people.

The little church was where they all gathered on Sunday to worship their God. The minister lived miles away in Cranton Section and serviced several churches on weekends. During the winter he often arrived at Murrays on Saturday evening by horse and wagon or sleigh. He spent the night and after service on Sunday morning he returned home, His name was Rev. MacPhail from Lake Ainslie. We were always happy to see him come as we enjoyed his many stories. There was no T. V. to entertain you in those days so story telling was great.

Winter came early that fall as Big Intervale is located at a high altitude, I can recall my shock when on Halloween day it began to snow. The children and I brought our lunch to school most days, depending upon the weather. Around 11 o'clock that morning it began to snow and snow and snow. No wind, just a soft snow fall. The children were somewhat disappointed as we planned to go trick or treating that evening. Around 3 :00 o'clock parents began to arrive with their horses and sleighs to bring the children home. Mr. Murray arrived to bring me home. That evening Mr. Murray asked me if I ever snow-shoed. I said "no." "Well, we have to teach you this evening because tomorrow morning you will have to snow shoe to school. I was amazed.

The Murrays had four (4) daughters who were all married and living in nearby areas. They adopted a little boy whose name was Jimmy. He was 14 years old. That evening Mr. Murray gave me a pair of snow shoes which belonged to his daughter Josie, we went out, Jimmy, Dan White and I. After a few tumbles I was able to walk on snow shoes. Sure enough, the next morning after all that night snow fall we were engulfed in mountains of snow. No roads! So over the fields Jimmy and I went. It was slow going as the snow was wet and sticky. We finally arrived at he school house and Jimmy built the fire in the little stove. I stood at a window and was amazed to see the children coming over the fields from every direction on snow shoes. Big smiles and pink noses, I met them at the door with lots of hugs. I was pleased to see how familiar they were with the situation. They took off their snow shoes, clapped them together to remove the snow and stood them in the hallway. Today kids park their bicycles or cars. Not these kids. The big surprise was seeing one little girl arriving. She had a problem walking and her father always drove Lauren and her brother Donnie to school, but that day she had a special limo. A beautiful Labrador Retriever was harnessed to a sled and he brought Donnie and Lauren to school. The dog was unharnessed and brought into the school where he spent the day receiving hugs and kisses. That was the daily routine. Everyone in the neighbourhood owned snow shoes. Once the snow settled the men cleared the road for horses and sleighs. There were no cars.

During the winter and long nights card games were played at various homes for past-time and, of course, the tea and goodies.

One evening Mr. & Mrs. Murray took me to visit Rod Y. MacKenzie and his wife. Rod Y. was a pipe major in the 1st World War. During the course of the evening he took out a souvenir he brought back from Scotland. He said it was a recording of a very special piece of Scottish music composed by a famous composer of Scottish music. Lo and behold, it was none other but Tulloch Gorm and played by Scott Skinner. We were all in awe. The record was a black thick disc. I have no idea where that recording is today as the MacKenzies have all passed away.

Another evening Mr. & Mrs. Murray took me to visit his cousin and wife whose name was also Dan Murray. They lived on top of a mountain. That visit brought to mind what living in Port Royal with Champlain's "Order of Good Cheer" must have been like. On that cold crisp moonlight night we reached the top of the mountain and entered a large flat plateau covered with snow. A tiny light led us to a log cabin where the Murrays lived. Going inside and being greeted by such loving, warm people was wonderful. The cabin consisted of one room with all the necessities. On the floor were bear skins used as rugs, a churn stood in the corner and a rifle was on the rack on the wall and a pair of hand made moccasins by the door. These people were happy and contented and would not change places for Buckingham Palace. They missed nothing and could teach us so much.

Winter finally ended and spring burst forth in all its glory. Trees began to blossom and flowers came into view. One day in mid May I told the children we were going on a field trip the next day. Instead of spending a beautiful afternoon in the classroom we would go out and explore nature's treasures. We walked quietly through the woods and the kids went crazy picking may flowers. What an aroma. I told them to be quiet or we would scare the animals away. Out of the clear blue sky we came across a mother deer nursing twin fawns. What a beautiful sight. Further down the river we saw a mother duck with a flock of baby ducks. We all enjoyed our field trip and the may flowers sent a lovely aroma through the school.

I finished my year in Big Intervale and became a better person. I went to Normal College the following year and taught for five (5) years in Nova Scotia. I came to Detroit in 1950, married and taught for another 22 years. I often told my students about my first year's experience and the little girl and the dog sled. They loved the story and yelled, Wow! I wish we could do that.

In closing I must say, "You can take a man out of the country, but you can't take the country from the man."

Mary White MacDougall
Northville, Michigan

(Let me insert a note here. I wrote Ms. MacDougall for permission to reprint this letter and she telephoned me back to say that she was more than happy for me to do so. We chatted a bit and she told she was raised in Fordview! Not only did she know all the people that we knew who were there when we came, but as a child she went to the one-room schoolhouse that was still going strong around 1960. Not only that, but Johnny Steven White, who we will encounter further on, was her uncle.)

The big change in those fifty years has been the consolidation into bigger and bigger schools. For most of that period the local consolidated school was in Margaree Forks. In the last five years or so there has been another big consolidation with new schools for a much bigger area: one in Mabou and one in Terre Noire. The Forks school has been closed down and demolished. There was tremendous resistance to this recent consolidation on the part of everyone in the vicinity, and felt especially strongly by the students at the Forks. Why change when everything was going so well? On various roads they put up S.O.S. (Save Our Schools) signs and wrote intelligent and heartfelt letters to the Oran. But the School Board forged ahead and built large new schools anyhow. It has always surprised me how often the government will do something that is so unpopular with the citizens and totally ignore public sentiment. Town hall type meetings will be held that are often resented by the local people because they rarely seem to change the government's mind; they are held for people to blow off steam and little more.

If one looks at the good and the bad of these consolidations, there are no doubt economic advantages that go with increase efficiency and these days that is always a vital consideration. As my grandfather used to say, "We can't afford it, so why talk about it?" Another argument in favor is that one can teach a greater diversity of subjects in larger schools. One unexpected good side effect of all this struggle–I am told by good authority–is that it brought the smaller communities together and gave them new vigor.

But there are disadvantages as well. For one, the students have very long bus rides. Those from Pleasant Bay take almost an hour and a half to get to Terre Noire, and the children in the Big Intervale have to be driven by a parent to Margaree Valley to catch the bus that takes almost a half hour to get to school. No more going on a sled pulled by a faithful dog.

The argument that a one room school house provides inferior education is an uncertain proposition. Think of all those men and women of a century ago started in one and became great politicians, great scholars, authors, actors, and almost everything else—and do not forget Anne of Green Gables! Is it possible that they instilled a greater desire to learn even though the menu they were offered was but a fraction of what is provided today? Perhaps some study has supplied an answer but I do not know it. And added to this is the irony that the number of young pupils in Cape Breton is decreasing now that the consolidation is in effect. Many families are moving west where there are greater opportunities for employment. Those marathon busses will have fewer and fewer young scholars to ride the weary miles.

Let me now turn to another matter that has undergone a dramatic change since we first came to Cape Breton. It is the roads; our main way of getting about in this age of automobiles. I have already described the dirt road that passed through Fordview; now I want to stress that it was no exception.

The main road between Rose's house and the barn. When the
new blacktop road was built it was on the other side
(the right side) of the barn.

The majority of the roads in the area were
dirt: blacktop roads were in the central parts of
the towns and made up the main highways. And
it was a standing joke that they were only resur-
faced—sometimes unnecessarily—just before elec-
tions. Even a drive to Baddeck or Sydney (a one
or two hour drive respectively, at least that is so
today with good roads all the way) involved long
stretches of dirt. These would shift from dirt to
blacktop abruptly, often at the border between two
counties (and when the change was from dirt to
blacktop, the feeling of palpable relief was overwhelming: like suddenly floating on a cloud). The
dirt roads have not gone: for instance there is still a
long stretch up river, between Margaree Valley and

the sparsely settled Big Interval (of the *Oran* letter). It, along with the other remaining dirt roads, are kept in fair shape, what with road scrapers and whole crews that come out to fix the damages of a sudden violent downpour that will flood and devastate a piece of the road.

A few years back for brief periods during the winter I have visited and then the road crews really have their work cut out for them after a blizzard. The whole countryside is glorious, covered in deep white; the Margaree river is quite covered in snow and ice, and in late winter the ocean is crunched up with solid ice, a spectacular sight driving along the shore road on a sunny day. I remember in our early days there reading in the local newspaper that a school bus full of children on their way home got hopelessly stuck in a blizzard by a farm and of course the farmer and his family took them all in, fed them and somehow put them all up for the night. Apparently as far as the children were concerned, it was the best school trip they had ever taken.

But not all the roads have improved. About thirty years ago I was fishing on the river, but faring poorly, with no sign of a salmon. I ran into another unsuccessful fisherman and we began to talk. It turned out he was an artist who painted the cover pictures for the venerable sporting magazine *Field & Stream*. We exchanged life histories and then he confessed he was having a rough time: his wife would barely speak to him. Apparently when he left the *Field & Stream* office to come north, a colleague said he had a old map of the Margaree area and gave it to him for the trip. They decided to explore a bit and spotted on the map a road that looked interesting from east to west between Grand Étang and the Big Intervale. The first seven miles went smoothly, but they gradually realized that the road was becoming rougher and rougher and looked less and less like a road. Eventually they could not even turn around and became irretrievably stuck. So they had to walk back the seven miles and his poor wife was wearing indoor shoes with heels. When they got back to Grand Étang to a garage that went to pull them out, they were not only exhausted but the old map put a dent in their harmony. There had indeed been such a road across the hills, but it had not exactly been kept up! The men at the garage thought it was very funny and assured them they were not the first; small consolation.

There were more ferries and fewer bridges in our earlier days. For instance to go to Sydney there was no Seal Island Bridge and one took the Ross ferry across the branch of the Bras D'Or the large inland sea (in Scotland it would be called a sea loch). One night I went across the island to pick up friends at the old Sydney airport and when we got back to the Bras d'Or at one in the morning, we could see the ferry on the other side. There was a big sign saying that to call the ferry after midnight we should press the bell in the middle of the sign.

It was pouring rain, and I dashed out and pressed it . Nothing happened, so we went out and pressed again. Considerably later we took a careful look at the bell from behind the sign and could see that there were no wires attached to it at all—it was just there to make one feel good. After about two hours the ferry came and we were rescued.

There are still a few ferries running today. One is further south also across a thin band of the Bras D'Or across the Little Narrows. It is a small ferry that carries a few cars and is very short ride. It used to cost 25 cents, but now it is 5 dollars. They keep the passageway open in winter and a friend told me that when she crossed a few winters back, two bald eagles were sitting on the ice just alongside and sedately walked along as the ferry progressed, which tells us something about the speed of the ferry. Presumably they were hoping for a handout. The other ferry still running is the Englishtown ferry which joins the west coast portion of the Cabot Trail to the eastern portion and the main road to Sydney. It is distinguished by being attached to a cable that runs a considerable distance across and down St. Ann's Bay. For the captain it must be rather like running a trolley car—no steering is involved, just the motion. On the old maps when we first came the waterway was called "St. Ann's Gut" which always seemed to me much more vivid than calling it a bay or a passage. The name had been neutered by some bureaucrat or politician.

When we first came trains were prevalent. One of their main uses were freight, in particular the moving of coal from the mines to the steel mills in Sydney. But the passenger traffic was considerable as well. In the 1960's we bought a lovely canvas covered wooden canoe which we found in one of those wonderful catalogues (I forget whether is was Eaton's or Montgomery Ward's, but I do remember that it was advertized as having been made by genuine Mohawk Indians!). We were told that it would be shipped to the station at Inverness where we could pick it up. The young were enthralled and we had some splendid times with it on the river. We still have it in the attic, but inevitably it was replaced by an aluminum canoe which, however practical, always looked seedy by comparison.

We sometimes went fishing for a few days in Quebec and we would take the train from Sydney or from Orangedale to Truro and beyond. The Orangedale station was a special treat. It was a lovely old building, and happily it has now been preserved as a museum. The thing I remember about it with particular fondness is that if passengers were boarding there the train had to be stopped. This was done by the stationmaster putting a wide board in brackets waist high right across the tracks which the train could see some distance ahead as it approached the station, and it dutifully came to a halt. No radio signals, no cell phones, just a board.

For passengers it seemed to me in those early days the station masters and the conductors were particularly friendly and helpful. I was coming back alone from a fishing trip in Quebec and the train was to reach Port Hawkesbury at something like two o'clock in the morning. I had a reservation in a motel a few miles back in Port Hastings. So I explained my predicament to the conductor and asked if there might be a taxi available at that hour in Port Hawkesbury because I had rather a heavy duffle with all my fishing gear. He said "no problem" and asked the name of the motel. He told me he would call me when the train stopped just below Skye Lodge Motel and all I had to do was walk up the hill. Only in Cape Breton could one find trains that drop you at your doorstep!

When we arrived with our old Jeep station wagon we needed to find a garage and were told that the Aucoin Garage in Grand Étang was a good place to go and indeed that turned out to be the case. The owner was Johnny Aucoin, a man of great charm and character. He was ably assisted by his son Victor and Packo Delaney. Going there for an oil change (or something more serious) was always a special event: one received more than one gave. In the first place Johnny made in very clear from the beginning that it was important not to hurry. He carried out this principle by periodically summoning me to sit down with him on an adjacent tire to discuss life. They often would be monologues on his past on the good old days. I remember one story which says a lot about Cape Breton and its people. He said in the winter time when he was younger upon occasion the whole family would pile in the sleigh and their horse would take them up that same old infamous road—then in good repair—from Grand Étang to the Big Intervale. In those early days the road had a number of farms along its winding way, and of course many of the families were relations or good friends. There were no telephones so one just burst in for a visit with no forewarning. They always got a big welcome and would stay for a few days—a bright spot for everyone in the middle of a long winter. After a story like this he would add with considerable scorn, "Today everything is rush, rush, rush." Except in Johnny's garage.

Victor's specialty was welding which he lovingly turned into an art. Once our tailpipe got bent in such a way that the exhaust fumes would come into the car. He made a new one for us that was a sight to behold with twists and turns like a French horn, and indeed the air was pure in the car and the tailpipe looked elegant. Packo was the master mechanic and he could solve any problem deep in the bowels of the machine, yet always accompanied with an amusing, self-deprecating banter. They also fixed boats, the lobster boats, and one day when I was there he was called out on an emergency: the boat motor would not start. Instead of grabbing his tools he got a roll of toilet paper and with a devilish smile he told me he knew exactly what was wrong. Sure enough he was back in five minutes; water had been shorting the spark plugs.

Today things are very different. There is no unseemly rushing in the garages; everything goes forward at a sensible pace. The biggest change is in the sophisticated machines for testing all aspects of the car's innards. Like a modern doctor there are all sorts of new testing devices. There are even specialists with very fancy equipment to do things such as test the wheel alignment. In the small, local garages there are still many first-rate mechanics and good diagnosticians. Like medical general practitioners they can fix most things, and if a specialist is needed they will guide you. Alas, the days of artistic welding are gone.

CHAPTER 3

During the winter of 1964 Rose told us she had rented the cabin to someone else so we had to scramble to find some other place. Fortunately there was a small house for rent in Margaree Harbour which we took.

It was owned by Tommy Ben MacDonald (of the mobile store) and his wife Christie. They ran a room and boarding house (MacDonald House) which was right next door. And one could not imagine better neighbors. Christie was a tall, solidly built person with a very strong personality. A few of her well chosen words and a characteristic nod of her head had a kind of finality to them: that was the way it was going to be. Yet beneath this firm exterior, she was a warm, thoughtful, and extremely intelligent person. What between her, and the cheerful Tommy Ben we could not have had better friends and neighbors. They both died a few years ago and it was a big loss to us and everyone.

Even though the house was small it was very much larger than the cabin!

Our house in Margaree Harbour.

There were three small bedrooms, a parlor, a large kitchen, and a good size bathroom with a noble bath-tub standing on four paws. It was all furnished in the simplest manner. The beds were old fashioned metal frames, the bureaus, the tables, the chairs were of the same simplest construction. And they all had a pleasant, used look. As I write these words they all surround me, much as they were when we first came.

We had decided to see if we could find a cabin that we could buy, so that we would not have the uncertainty of not finding a place for the coming summers. We were casting about with little success when one day Tommy Ben came in to see me.

Tommy Ben with his beloved Bessie off to manure the garden.

He said, "Mr. Bonner, I hear you are looking for a place to buy." (In those days no one would call us by our first names, despite the fact that we were young. Special pleading was of no avail. Nowadays everybody is identified by their first name, which I rather like.) I agreed that we were indeed looking for a cabin. He said, "Why don't you buy this house?" I replied, "Tommy Ben, I could not possibly afford it. I'm just a beginning professor and I have a growing family." He smiled and answered, "Maybe you can. I have two prices: one for people we don't want as neighbors, and one for people we do." We felt the compliment deeply and he made an offer we indeed could not refuse. I still am in that old house. It was the best thing that ever happened to us.

And it is an old house. I have never been able to find out exactly how old, but Hastings Laurence at the store—our local historian—told me years ago that it was one of the two oldest houses in the village of Margaree Harbour. My guess is that it was probably built in the early 1800's. What is more, while it has undergone some modifications over the years, the initial basic structure is there and still visible. Some of the other old houses have undergone many renovations to keep out the winter cold, such as modern insulation, metal or plastic siding, elegant flooring, and so forth. Our house still has the old wooden clapboards, mostly the old wooden floors, and the only insulation between the outside and inside wooden walls is a layer of birch bark.

Presumably it seals the wind out. I asked a visiting friend of one of my sons about it, who is an energy engineer who studies how to build heat-conserving houses. He said there are much better ways to insulate, but according to Tommy Ben nothing matched birch bark. All the walls had many layers of wall paper that had accumulated over the years which certainly made some contribution to keeping out the cold. We have systematically scraped it all off, and now one can see the old boards, each of varying widths, and showing signs on the back of the saw of the sawmill, and on the fronts where the surface was smoothed with a drawknife.

The price was so reasonable that we decided we could afford some modifications. There was a huge attic at the back of the house that the children immediately discovered by crawling through a small hatch. We engaged the local carpenter, Duncan MacDonald, and he put in a proper door and a floor. He also converted the shed at the back of the house, off the kitchen, into our living room: wooden walls to replace, or cover, the newspaper glued to the inside of the outer walls, and put in a large store front picture window which gives us a glorious view over the estuary of the Margaree river and Belle Côte and the hills beyond. The old parlor in the front of the house became the coat room, the rod and fishing gear room, and later also the piano room, and much later, the laundry room. The house was obviously modified some time after it was built: the whole portion that is under the attic was added on. There are two ship's knees in the corners that connect the new part to the old, presumably so the wind would not blow it away.

We did have a slight problem with the old water pump that kept breaking down. We had a pipe down Tommy Ben's well and we shared his water. When the pump failed Tommy Ben would come over and encourage it to get going again. (He always told me of his deceased friend Jimmy Jim who could think like a motor and fix the worst cases in no time.) Another problem was that if the MacDonald house had a number of guests, suddenly we would start sucking in air and no water, and the frustrated pump would keep going. I would wake up in the middle of the night, rush down to the cellar and turn it off.

Finally, one day Christie came over and announced firmly, as only she knew how: we had to dig a new well, ending with that nod of her head which was her way of punctuating the end of a paragraph. We engaged a well digger and that was the worst period of all our years up here. The machine came and it was gigantic—taller than the house. I looked out right at it from my study and while I stuck to my morning quota of words I wonder if they were not blighted. To add to my torture I knew every foot of digging had a price so every day I saw myself going deeper into bankruptcy. The final straw was that the incredibly noisy diesel engine shot its exhaust straight at the house so we were all being poisoned by concentrated smelly pollution. I felt this was the ultimate test: I could do my writing no matter what. And then we put a Jacuzzi pump at the bottom of the new, 100 foot well and have entered the soft, modern world. For the first time the bath filled with the speed of one in a Hilton hotel.

There was another aspect of houses in general that has changed over the years. It is their general appearance from the outside. Today most of the houses are brightly painted, or more often covered with well kept siding. They were very different in early days. The once colorful paint on many of the houses in the whole area showed the signs of having been savaged by the weather with patches where the paint was gone. Also the decorations around the houses have undergone a radical transformation. When we first came there was common to see a branched support on the front lawn holding a number of empty plastic Javex jugs that have been cut in such a way that there were little open doors all around the middle. A round dowel was driven into the ground, the Javex bottle placed upside down on the dowel. These would catch the wind and spin the jug merrily in the breeze. And there were no flowers around the house. We had a friend from Scotland visit us and he was quite disturbed by this: how could a land with so many Scots not plant flowers in their yards? I assured him there were exceptions and showed him a house where the short drive had flowers on each side: they were artificial flowers all neatly arranged in two rows of discarded automobile tires. How different it is today. Every house has an impressive array of beautiful flowers around them. I am always particularly affected by the common sight of hollyhocks along the side of a house (and not a Javex jug to be seen).

When we came, as in all rural communities, there were local telephone operators with a board in their kitchen. In fact, our local telephone board was in MacDonald House, and Tommy Ben and Christie's daughter Catherine was in charge of it and had a number of local women taking turns managing it during the day. This is something everyone misses. There was a human face to the machinery. To give an example, we were out one evening to friends for dinner and Andrew and Jeremy were alone in the house. They were about 10 and 14 at the time. We decided to call them to be sure they were going to bed so I rang our house giving the operator our number (Margaree Harbour 23). The bell rang and rang with no answer. Suddenly a voice came on, I think it was Georgina, saying they don't answer. I identified myself and said I was just checking if the boys were OK. She said, "I'm sure they are: I can see a light in Jeremy's room." I was relieved and thanked her, but after I hung up I wondered how she knew which was Jeremy's bedroom! Our son Jonathan told me he once called us at about 10:00pm EST. He had forgotten about the one hour time difference so it was 11pm in Margaree. The operator, Catherine MacDonald, answered and he said to her "can you please ring Margaree Harbour 23." Catherine, recognizing his voice said "Jonathan, you can't call them now, they're asleep!" Another time a friend called someone up and the voice intervened saying, "I don't think Mrs. Bogart is in; I saw her driving towards the Forks." Those were the good old days.

But all was not that perfect: there were party lines that have little to recommend them. By some lucky chance we did not have one, but the tales from friends were without end. There were four or more phones on the same line and the call was for you if you heard the right number of rings, which required patience and attention. If more than one person answered then the voice became weaker and more remote. We were visiting Margret MacLeod (the widow of the esteemed Dr. MacLeod) at Lake Ainslie some years ago and her daughter was a biochemist working in a research hospital in London, England and periodically would call her mother in Cape Breton. The difficulty was that the others on the party line were so fascinated to hear a voice from across the Atlantic that they would pick up their receivers to listen in. Margaret immediately knew that was happening because suddenly her daughter's voice became very faint. So she would bark over the phone, "Would everyone please get off the line, so I can hear my daughter." The command was obeyed, followed by the clicking of the phones hanging up, and a voice she could hear again. Many of the telephones then still had to be hand cranked to get on the line.

I had a dear friend, Dr. Edwards Park, who lived in sort of a camp that he had built close to the river in Northeast Margaree. For many years he had been the head of the pediatrics department of John Hopkins Medical School and since his retirement he would spend even more time fishing for salmon on his beloved Margaree river. He never had a telephone in his modest camp, but when his wife became quite ill, and he was well into his 80's his children insisted he get a phone. This was still in the days of telephone operators, and he was admired and loved for all he had done, as a volunteer, for the health of the children in the valley. So his phone was installed and they gave him the telephone number of Margaree Forks 1. I immediately called him up to congratulate him on this great honor which he clearly appreciated. He went on to say that when he started his medical practice in New York City as a young man his telephone number was Murray Hill 7. The world has changed, not only in New York, but in Cape Breton as well.

Music has always been part of our children's lives. Both Ruth and I were deficient; neither of us could play an instrument (although she had a true voice), but we loved to listen. Andrew was a precocious pianist and continues to play today. He and Becky, his wife, who is a superb cellist, are masters of classical music. Jeremy used to play the drum in a small band with friends, and now he sings soft songs to himself on to the guitar. During college Jonathan became a ardent devotee of Cape Breton music and taught himself how to play the violin, showing remarkable zest and technical skill. He can play tunes such as Killekrankie and make me melt inside. And now his young daughter, Ondine, has become infected and is making remarkable progress, with total enthusiasm. When we are all together in the house in the summer the place is vibrating.

At the time Andrew was about eight and wanted to practice his piano we were in a quandary; we had no instrument. We found someone in the village who said he could practice on hers, but that did not last long for reasons we never fully understood (We suspected because he played with greater facility than the owner.) So we asked permission of the church elders if he could practice on the church organ and the answer was a firm NO; no small child could be wandering around the church. We mentioned this to some old friends and they were immediately furious for they had donated to organ to the church. They said "we'll see about this," and presto, permission was granted. There was one condition attached: an adult had to be with him while he practiced, and that turned out to be me. So I would join him sitting on a very hard pew with a book. The organ had fewer keys than the piano, so if Andrew had to hit the upper, absent notes he just played on the wood with his fingers—it did not seem to hold him back at all. During those sessions I made a significant scientific discovery. The stained glass windows consisted of panels of different colors, and the house flies trying to escape to the outside seemed to accumulate on the purple glass; they imagined that was the doorway to their freedom.

We finally decided, despite our impoverished bank book, that we had to get a piano and found that McKnight's, the music store in Sydney, sold second hand pianos. Andrew tried them all out and finally found one with the best action. It was an old upright but it worked and had an interesting honky-tonk quality to its tone. They delivered it into the old parlor—our fishing stuff and everything else room—and Andrew was in heaven. Very shortly after it came, he discovered that under the keyboard there must have been over a hundred fossilized bits of parked chewing gum which we spent some time scraping off. I do not remember if the gum added or hindered the quality of the tone. The piano is still going strong to this day.

Many years later, when Andrew started coming each summer with his talented wife Becky we had to see if we could find a cello for a few weeks. I spent some hours on the phone being passed from one person to another and finally reached Otis Tomas at St. Ann's who lent us one that he had made.

I found out Otis was a friend of Jonathan and they met in a most interesting Cape Breton way. Jonathan and his family live in Providence, Rhode Island, and Otis and was visiting his parents there. He and his wife Deany were busking on a street corner with their violins. As Jonathan drove by with his window open he suddenly heard a Cape Breton tune: *Glencoe March*! He quickly parked his car, rushed back, borrowed Deany's violin and joined Otis in the tune. Music was the bond to Cape Breton and to a good friendship. Otis is a master luthier and made both Jonathan's violin and Becky's cello, both superb instruments.

Otis and Deany Tomas were among the many Americans who came to Canada to escape the horrors and wrong-headedness of the Vietnam war. It was part of the young people's revolution everywhere, but was particularly virulent in the States because of the war. A number of Americans migrated north and some of those came to the Margaree in the late 1960s and early 70s. There was even a commune up Big Brook road, entirely populated by Canadians from Winnipeg, and smaller groups scattered elsewhere. They were regarded by the local Cape Bretoners with wonderment mixed with amusement and some sympathy. At that time Jonathan had long hair and Jeremy a full beard. They were going down the river in the canoe and passed a group of fishermen at a large pool and they got a smiling cheer from the bank: "HIPPIES." The immigrants have turned out for the most part to be stellar citizens: the United States' loss has been Canada's gain.

* * * *

More on music in Cape Breton
by Jonathan Bonner

The first several years that we came to Margaree, I was completely unaware that there was such a thing as Cape Breton music. The first couple of summers were spent hanging out with the Miller kids (Anne, Mary, Gerard and Lawrence) and the Greg Tompkins kids (Genevieve and Paul). Then salmon fishing took over and most of my time was spent on the river. When I was in college in the late 60's a bunch of us including my good friends Ansell and Dina Bray from New York, landed at the Beatons of Broad Cove Marsh – John Allen and his wife Margie, their seven children and John Allen's brother Alex. The three grownups were Gaelic speakers. We entered their kitchen and the kettle was put on the stove and sandwiches were served. John Allen brought out the violin and began to play. It was like nothing that I had ever heard. He was not a fancy player but he truly had the music. The rhythm, the Scotchyness, the overwhelming sense of soul – it just blew me away. It was a true expression of culture. The music was not delivered from performer to audience but rather belonged to everyone in the room.

From that moment on, I began to chase the music. At about this time my then girl friend, now wife Jacqueline gave me a violin for my birthday and I started to learn to play. The most amazing discovery was that fact that many of the people in Margaree that I knew were involved with the music. First and foremost was Johnny Steven White. I had seen him on a daily basis for years, either on the river or at Rose Tompkin's mail call. It turns out he was a fiddler and composer of tunes and taught the great Angus Chisholm from Margaree Forks his first tune. Angus's brother Archie Neil Chisholm lived in Margaree Forks. I had met him because we used to park in his driveway when fishing the Big MacDaniel pool and had been in for tea and a lunch from his wife Margaret.

Shortly after meeting the Beatons I went to the Broad Cove Concert that was MC'd by Archie Neil. I went to visit him shortly afterwards told him that I was interested in Scotch Music. He got out his fiddle and played for an hour or so. He was a left handed fiddler. He had really good timing and was great at a dance. Archie Neil suggested that I visit his nephew Cameron Chisholm. I went to see Cameron who also lives in Margaree Forks with his father Willie D and his mother Annie Mae. This house was jam packed with music. Cameron is one of the all time great Cape Breton violin players. His sister Mae Belle is one of the all time great Cape Breton piano players. Sister Margaret is also an amazing player.

At that time they had a border, Sandy Boyd from Largs in Ayershire, Scotland. He was a master piper, classically trained with a tremendous repertoire. Willie D and Annie Mae would not allow Sandy to play the pipes down stairs because of the volume. The Highland War pipes were not made for playing in the parlor. When I wanted to hear him play, we would go into his room and close the door. The room was about a foot wider than his bed. We would sit next to each other and he would play away, for as long as I could stand it. Every particle that made up Sandy Boyd was there for the music.

It was impossible for a musician to enter that house without Annie Mae insisting that they play a tune. At Willie D's and Annie Mae's I met many other musicians including Gordon Cote, his young son Dwayne from Grande Greve and Dougie MacDonald from Queensville. It was there that I first met Jerry Holland and his parents. When I first met him, he was 16. He had been a prodigy and was already a veteran of the Cape Breton music scene, both in Boston and Cape Breton. Jerry had a great influence among Cape Breton musicians. He was a sweet player who composed hundreds of great tunes. He was always very encouraging of other players especially the younger ones. He and his parents lived in Terre Noire. Jerry later moved to Belle

Côte and then to Margaree Harbour and became our neighbor.

The other person that I got to know quite well was Johnny Murphy who lived up towards Lake a law in Northeast Margaree. I first met him because I was pulled in by his sign "Musical Instrument Museum". He and his wife Hilda had many instruments that were hung up on the walls of his living room. They included fiddles, auto harps, Ukelines, mandolins and even an alpine horn. On more than one occasion we took that one out in the yard and gave her a blast (much to the chagrin of the Hannigans next door). Johnny's favorite tune was Sandy's Dream, which he could play on many of the instruments (not the alpine horn). Johnny was a wonderful storyteller. It was a treat to listen to him talk about Margaree in the old days.

* * * *

CHAPTER 4

The Mi'kmaq people are quite rightly referred to as the First Nation. They were the only inhabitants of Cape Breton for thousands of years before the Europeans arrived. As is true of that foreign invasion, and of the invasions of all the Americas, right from the beginning there was an almost total refusal to grant the invaded any rights: they were the conquered people. And worse they had different customs, different languages, and different religions: they were heathens. While it is true that the Mi'kmaqs of Nova Scotia were first converted to Catholicism some 400 years ago, they largely have not abandoned their own beliefs, and even their Catholic rituals bear their special imprint.

There has been a big change throughout the new world in our attitude towards native peoples, especially over the last 50 years. There has been a slow realization that we have treated them abdominally as second class, essentially non-citizens, for centuries. (In Canada they only formally became citizens in 1957.) We made land treaties with them and as our population increased broke these treaties without a scintilla of remorse. We Europeans treated them with either avoidance or contempt, and the conviction that the only solution was to recreate them into our own image. As a result children of all ages were taken by both the United States and Canadian governments, removed from their families, sometimes at an early age and placed in religious boarding schools where they were forbidden to speak their own language. It was a cruel measure and only made the situation worse. It is hard to believe that in Canada those schools were only disbanded in the 1960's, just shortly after our arrival in Cape Breton. All over the world there has been a slow appreciation of the fact that other cultures have their own virtues and should certainly be preserved. In Cape Breton they hung on by a thin thread, although today their language is mostly (but not universally) preserved.

What I have noticed in our years here is that our friends and neighbors have gradually become more tolerant of the natives and their culture. I think there is still a long way to go but there is movement in the right direction. Perhaps it is a misguided theory on my part, but I have a suspicion that the prime event behind this change in Cape Breton is the Marshall case. In Sydney, Donald Marshall, Jr., the son of a chief, and a friend, both in their 20's, got into a fight with another man and his companion was stabbed to death. The trial was a travesty loaded with prejudice that produced false testimony, withheld evidence, and finally was totally repudiated in an appeal in 1983. But by then Marshall had spent 11 years in prison for a crime he did not commit. This produced a sort of revolution, or perhaps I should say revulsion, not only in legal circles, but in the minds of the citizens of Cape Breton. This was raw injustice produced by racial prejudice; all Cape Bretoners were affected by the "Marshall affair."

Since their beginnings thousands of years ago, and in the early treaties made with the new settlers, the natives had the right to take game, such as deer and salmon. This was their land. With the great population increase of non-natives game laws were instituted: fishing and hunting licenses had to be bought, there were restricted seasons and bag limits imposed by patrolling wardens. Then a few years ago, much to the horror of sportsmen, the Mi'kmaq challenged the law: it did not apply to them as agreed in the original treaty with the first settlers. They won their old rights back in court—they had the right to kill as many beasts as they needed for themselves, and at any time of year. Consternation! The rivers would be denuded of salmon and the deer would vanish. Soon after the new law was passed a large group of native fishermen descended on the Margaree river off season with great fanfare.

I no longer remember how many fish they caught (I think it was rather few), but they made a pointed lesson. To the amazement of the observers, they released every one and calm was restored. Sportsman began to see that in the native culture, conservation was one of their basic tenets and they had been practicing it for eons.

I do not say that all prejudice has gone, but there certainly has been vast progress in the last 50 years.

I was fortunate in that in the early 2000's to be able to visit some of the reservations. A good friend was part of a program that was run by Cape Breton University for native students who wanted credits towards a college degree. She would visit a reservation for a few weeks and give an intensive, all-day, every day course on a variety of subjects, and on a few occasions I would accompany her and sit in with the classes. There were usually about one to two dozen students, but what was remarkable was their composition. The women outnumbered the men, and their age ranged from young 20's to grandmothers, including an occasional Elder, a most lofty title. They were respectful, and for the most part attentive.

One of my friend's major challenges was to relate western notions to the Mi'kmaq philosophy and traditions. For this she read extensively of native lore such as creation of the universe and other fundamental matters. Being a physicist she would, for instance, compare and contrast those ancient Mi'kmaq concepts with modern cosmology, And she did the same for other subjects, such as medicine so that their vision was expanded and they could see where they fit in with the ideas of the outside world. They were likely to be far more receptive to new ideas than if the were simply told that their revered ones were wrong and had to be abandoned. They learned where they fit in with other civilizations.

If it was a science class she would ask me to talk for a bit on some biological subject, and I felt a responsive and interested audience. Once in a final session, when everyone was saying goodbye, they gave me a little present, a beaded necklace with "John" spelled out in beads, and the native supervisor of the course gave me a big hug and kissed me! In all my years of teaching at Princeton University nothing like that had ever happened!

At another ending of a school week the native organizer presented me with a book that she said had been written by her grandfather. It was called, "We were not the Savages" by Daniel Paul. It is an appalling indictment of the way the Mi'kmaq were treated.

Also through my friend I got to know Albert Marshall, an Elder on the Eskasoni reservation. He and his wife Murdena are remarkable people. He travelled widely in his younger days and is a master at public meetings, carrying the day with perfect timing; an eloquent champion of Mi'kmaq lore. I asked him what were the qualifications to become an Elder, which he explained in detail and at some length. They involved a large number of virtues and other fine qualities. I knew right then I could never achieve the exalted status of an Elder no matter how many years I lasted.

There is another matter—quite unrelated–that also bears on Cape Breton in a big way and has gone through seismic changes in the last fifty years. When we first came, coal mining was a major industry in Cape Breton. There were many mines on the east coast in the Sydney area and a few near us on the west coast near Mabou and St. Rose, and right in the town of Inverness, less than a half hour drive from us. To the casual visitor Inverness was a very different town then than it is now; the mine there has been closed for some time. My first recollection were great hilly areas between the town and the ocean covered with what looked grey gravel that had come to the surface along with the coal. There was the train yard with freight cars full of coal. And there were mines on the other side of town as well.

One of the most striking features was the coal dust everywhere in town: all the side walks were grey with it, and even the houses were covered with a thin layer of black powder. By comparison, today, with coal mining long past, Inverness is bright and shiny. The grey hills are becoming green and the side walks immaculate. There are still some reminders of the coal days; its traces have not been completely obliterated. Along the main street there is still a row of the half houses—two houses stuck together—that the coal company had constructed for its workers, and there are still places at the edge of town that show the scars of the mining of yore.

When we first came there was another sight to touch the tender heart. The mines were only partially mechanized, and much of the work down below involved pit ponies. But August was a holiday for all mining and the pit ponies were brought to the surface and allowed to gamble on green pastures for a whole month. Then back to their eternal darkness until the next August.

In those early days we knew a number of miners who suffered from black lung and were retired on a pension. Some of them had cabins on the Margaree and were, or became, master fishermen. It was a disease that could become devastating in its effects—the coal particles stayed and accumulated in the lungs and for that reason there is little hope of repairing the damage. It was not just the ponies, but all those thousands of miners who led a very hard life; some good things came when all the mines in Cape Breton were closed. To fully appreciate the harshness of a miner's existence there is nothing comparable to watching a profoundly moving film, *Margaret's Museum,* which came out in 1995. It is not for the faint hearted.

It also tells the story of the company store that made miners serfs of the coal mine owners. Their elimination occurred some time before we came, but its effect is still evident. Fathers Moses Coady (1882-1959) and Jimmy Tompkins (1870-1953) were key promoters of the Cooperative movement (the COOP) so that the miners owned the store and where company money, part of the serfdom, was pushed into oblivion and replaced by real dollars. The two were remarkable men who rightfully have become Cape Breton heroes today, but of course before our time.

I did know Dr. Tompkins, a cousin of Rose Tompkins, who knew his illustrious relative. Father Tomkins told him the following story, which says nothing about miners, but does tell us a little something of the man. Whatever parish he had, he promoted literacy: he urged his parishioners to borrow books from his own library, and he taught as many as he could reach to read and write. One day he went back to a previous parish where he had served and met an older man in the street who had taken those literacy lessons with him. He hailed him and asked whether he had benefitted from learning how to read, and the answer was an enthusiastic, "Yes, it was wonderful: now I can play Bingo!"

The serious consequence of all the coal mines and the steel plant in Sydney was that when they all closed down, after we had been here some years, they left behind an enormous amount of pollution. The scars of many of the mines to a small degree have been muted by grass, but the tar ponds in Sydney, as the deposits of the steel-making refuse is called, are a wound that will not heal despite great efforts to get rid of them—a long time is needed. One might argue that these are small blemishes on such a large island, but still they are the sore thumb that stands out.

A few years ago there was a great stir when the waters off both coasts of Cape Breton were sold to companies to explore for oil. This was a big issue and those who wanted it for economic reasons considered the objections of the environmentalists anti-progress. Those objections were in part because it would be a blight on our beautiful seascapes, and perhaps risky because of oil leaks. The letters in the Oran, the local newspaper, blazed fury from both sides. The areas were nevertheless sold for exploration, but in the intervening years nothing has happened, so all is quiet.

There was a similar flurry of excitement when a gold mining company planned to set up operation in the National Park, but here public opinion was strongly opposed and worried about the trucking roads that would invade the Park and the danger of polluting the Margaree river. They prevailed and the plan was abandoned.

There was a more extended tempest in the 1970's when the great spruce forests became infested with the spruce bud worm, which is fatal to the trees. There were two opposing sides: those who said spray to kill the pest and those who said let nature take its course. There are some problems with spraying: one cannot stop doing it; it must go on for years, and it kills other insects which greatly affects the bird population. And it was a danger to the people who were near or in the Park.

Nevertheless the pulp paper company was, for obvious reasons, strongly in favor of spraying. The other view is that spruce budworm infestation runs in cycles and is bound to peter out of its own accord. The Province did a bit of spraying and then finally stopped. The loss of trees was very large, but it has recovered. Now a new pest, a bark beetle, is killing the spruce but there has been no spraying; just dismay as one stares at the dead trees on the hills.

In our first years here the great fort built by the French from 1720 to 1740 was no more than a pile of rubble. It had been systematically destroyed by the conquering British in 1758. The early 1960's was still a time of economic upheaval in Cap Breton and there was a distressingly large number of unemployed miners. To provide jobs, for at least some, an ambitious program was launched to restore the old fortress. Fortunately all the architectural details and much additional information about Louisbourg still existed in the archives in Paris; it was possible to make a very exact replication of about one fourth of the original fort. It was a remarkable achievement and today stands as one of the finest living museums in the world. The details include the soldiers blankets, carefully duplicated, the restaurants, the furniture in the commandant's elegant quarters, the bread, which was the soldiers daily ration (which is still made from the original recipe and sold to the visiting tourists), and many other things. What impressed me most was how favorably it compared to the restoration of the colonial Williamsburg in the United States that I visited once. The buildings are equally successful, but not in the details. I was taken to the restaurant in Williamsburg and the food was the same as any restaurant in town, the candles were electric, and the waitress, while wearing appropriate colonial clothes, wore bat-wing glasses with rhinestones. In Louisbourg the menu is the original 18th century one (and delicious), the napkins clearly authentic (they were the size and texture of baby's diapers when they were still made of cloth), and the waitress's glasses had rectangular frames, just like those of Benjamin Franklin. Louisbourg won hands down.

Local weekly newspapers have existed here for many years. When we came it was the *Victoria-Inverness Bulletin* which expired in 1969 and was replaced by the *Inverness Oran* in 1976. Our first encounter with the Bulletin was one of fascination: it all seemed so different from the *New York Times* which was our daily fare in Princeton. Of course it only dealt with local news, and to us ignorant outsiders it seemed refreshingly different. I devoured it and learned many things about the local community. Even the advertisements were read with close attention and I learned who had a second hand wood stove for sale, or who was looking for a used washing machine. The news included all sorts of interesting things such as where to find concerts or dances filled with Cape Breton music. I was particularly affected by the obituaries because they were often accompanied by touching poems that were remarkably well written. It was only a few years later that I was disillusioned by mentioning this to a newspaper editor in South Carolina who laughed at my ignorance. He told me that every country newspaper has a book of poems from which the bereaved can choose. So much for all those thousands of poets of Cape Breton, but they do have a few gifted ones but they do not write for the newspapers.

I have another special memory of *Victoria-Inverness Bulletin*. In one issue a small squib was inserted in the middle of a page with other brief items. I do not remember the exact wording, but it announced that two Confederate spies had been hanged for their sins by the Union military. The United States civil war had been over for almost a hundred years: a newspaper is supposed to have the latest! But then I was told by a pro that country newspapers keep small items at hand if a space needs to be filled. Some wag in the office of the *Bulletin* had found this one and decided to have some fun—and he succeeded!

After a hiatus of a few years the *Bulletin* was followed by the *Inverness Oran* which to this day I read equally faithfully every week when I am here. Today the *Oran* has more pages, photographs in color, and a number of added features, but in essence it is a very similar newspaper. It has some regular columns of different degrees of interest, the news of the local musical world, a spirited section on local sports from ju-jitsu, to school athletics, to horse racing—trotting—at the Inverness track. It has a medical column of considerable interest and mini-sermons from the local churches.

For me, on occasion, by far the most riveting can be the letters to the editor, especially when there is a raging controversy. This happened just a few years ago when the government announced that it was going to designate the Margaree river a Heritage River. No one quite understood what this meant: some imagined that this was just a name, rather like putting a plaque on an old house saying it was a historic building; others imagined it was a government take over of their beloved river. They were the ones that wrote the furious letters to the *Oran*. They were strong stuff, usually well written, and riveting reading. Eventually the Margaree did become a Heritage River and indeed all is peaceful, there have been no changes, and there has not been a squeak about it in the *Oran*. After is all subsided I asked a friend why the whole affair had raised such passions, and the answer, to me as a outsider, was very interesting. The Cape Breton Highlands National Park, which lies to the north of the river valley was established in 1936. In all ways it is a splendid park, but its establishment was the cause of great anger and distress. All those who lived within the new Park boundaries were evicted which obviously created great unhappiness among the victims and all their sympathizers in the rest of the island. And there were many who still had the scars: it was their great fear that the Heritage River status would lead to similar tragedies. Fortunately it has not.

Other lively letters were also sometimes perceived governmental outrages, or on matters of religion, and of course, politics. There was a particularly heated exchange when one of the local pastors wrote a column in which he said that homosexuality was a sin. This produced a hot response pointing out that the modern world held a different view.

CHAPTER 5

B esides the improvements in the telephone, there are a number of mechanical inventions that have had a profound impact on the whole world and, of course, Cape Breton as well. Many of them are trivial, but locally they have taken on special meaning. Just the other day we were motoring up to the Big Intervale and the dirt road was dry and very dusty. We came behind another car that surrounded us with an impressive dust storm, so we closed all the windows and turned on the air conditioner. Our vision was not great, but the air we breathed was more-or-less pure. In early days we just suffered, or stopped and just let the other car get well ahead of us. And one of the great things about Cape Breton that we never felt the need, or even thought of, air conditioning in the house.

Television arrived during our fifty years here, and I believe (although these are my casual observations and not a serious sociological study) that its effect has been profound. When we first came I had the very distinct impression that women's styles in their dresses and that their hair cuts were distinctly different from what I was used to south of the border. Even the young teen age girls and certainly the older women looked rural. I rather liked the simplicity of it, but it was definitely something new for me. But then television crept in with ever increasing popularity and everything changed. Gradually all the Cape Breton women looked like the Princeton women (and all the women on television!). I do not know if this homogenization of the world is good or bad, but the fact that it did change is inescapable. And a further unscientific observation. There were even some changes in language. When we first came I remember if I said to a young person something like, "What a lovely day," the reply would be, "Is it ever," which always delighted me. But I hear it rarely now. A few summers ago my son showed one of the local families a video of my granddaughter Ondine playing the fiddle. The young daughter of the family said "Ondine, are you ever good to play," which I am told is a direct translation from Gaelic.

When Tommy Ben and Christie got their first television for their boarding house, the telephone linesmen used to stay there if they were working in the area. One day I was looking out my kitchen window and could see that they had put an old fashioned antenna high up on the telephone pole. One man stood at its base with a great claw-like device with which he could rotate the whole pole. He would move it a bit and yell. "Any better," and the muffled response within the house who were monitoring the sharpness of the picture on the screen, would give a yell back, "Try it a bit further." Cape Bretoners have this wonderful gift of solving all problems in the most efficient and least compli-cated way.

Computers and communication through satel-lites have changed the world and Cape Breton along with it. Paying at the market with a credit card that instantly removes money from your bank was unimaginable just a few years back. And shopping on line too. I notice it most in my summer writing. I used to write out everything out longhand on a yellow pad (with the help of scissors and glue) and mail the mess to a secretary in Princeton. That splen-did person was a genius at reading my handwriting and soon I would get back a beautiful typed version (the mail was faster in those days), I would correct it, mail it back; the poor secretary had to type the whole thing all over and again mail it. What a change now: here I am sitting before my laptop typing out some-thing that looks more like a printed version than a manuscript. And I can read it: most (but not all!) of my errors instantly hit me between the eyes.

I have one regret that came with the advance-ment of technology, but it is a mild one. Some years back the power company decided it would be profitable and a public service to put street lights in the villages. In Margaree Harbour we used to be able to see the magical array of stars at night, but that, alas, is gone; we have light pollution The only time we recover the night is when there is a power outage. But then there is the advantage that when I have to go to the bathroom in the middle of the night no flashlight is needed.

One final point on the fringe of technology. When we came it was miles, gallons and Fahrenheit; now it is kilometers, liters, and centigrade. I am all in favor of the metric system and never cease to wonder that my country, the United States, was so conservative and backward that it did not make the change. As far as these measures are concerned I have become, like all of us, bilingual.

The importance of the mail is declining today because of competition from fast carriers, and particularly from e-mail, but it is still very important. It is simply a more modest player in everybody's lives. The number of small, rural post offices has declined, but far from gone. Fordview no longer has a post office of its own; were Rose Tompkins still alive she would not be the Post Mistress. Rose's daily mail call was quite an event when the mail truck pulled up with the mail. About 10 to 15 people would walk in for a few miles from Arsenault Hill on one side and from Doyles Bridge on the other. The bundle of mail would be opened by Rose and she would call out the mail letter by letter, package by package. (When we would leave at the end of the summer, in those early days, and say goodbye to Rose, her response to, "We'll see you next summer," was always, "Oh, I don't know: I may be under the sod.")

Margaree Harbour had a permanent, full time post master. When we first came it was Tim Burns, an elf with a twinkle in his eye, and definitely a bit of the devil in him. I remember one Saturday after his closing time and on his way, he pulled up his car by the house where we were standing and said, with a satanic grin, "Oh, Mr. Bonner I have a Special Delivery letter for you: you can pick it up on Monday." That was Tim's idea of special delivery, and he got a big charge out of it. He ruled his kingdom his way.

He was succeeded by Marion Timmons who was a generous and splendid person, and a good neighbor, loved by the whole village. A cheery voice over the counter. In Princeton, in the laboratory, I work with lowly organisms called slime molds, and in the 1980's the BBC did a documentary in my lab that was also shown in Canada by David Suzuki in an episode of his *The Nature of Things* series. When I returned to Margaree Harbour the following summer, Marion said to me across the counter how much she enjoyed the show: "It was like having you in the living room." But then she went on to say she found slime molds both repulsive and frightening. We talked for a while and it dawned on me that she had not realized the slime mold films were taken through a microscope; She thought they were my size, and that I was like St. George and the dragon. I did not quite convince her that slime molds were lovable, but at least not life threatening.

Russell Timmons was Marion's husband; they lived right across the road from us and many a time we would join them around their kitchen table for a chat. Marion was full of interesting things about her youth in nearby Smithville and Russell had a great fund of amusing stories. He came from up the valley and drove a huge pulp truck which by some miracle he was able to back into their small driveway with incredible precision every evening. And he was off to work at three in the morning. He was full of good stories. He told us how he had been born prematurely, but been saved because his mother had put him in a shoe box behind the stove—an early incubator baby. And he had a wonderful way of telling a story using plenty of Irish color. He and Marion had been to a fiddle concert the night before and he came over to our house to tell us about it. One of the players was a small boy who showed remarkable talent, and Russell describe him as a brilliant performer despite his size, "for I'm telling you, John, he was no bigger than my cat,"

The period of consolidation of the Post Offices was one of anger and distress for many. There were town meetings where the matter was discussed with officials. It was a splendid opportunity for everyone could blow off steam, and who knows how the political-bureaucratic mind works, but the end result seemed to satisfy most people. Many of the villages kept a Post Office: in Margaree Harbour, it became incorporated into the General Store, and Fletcher Laurence has done a splendid job carrying the torch.

In earlier days the Canadian customs were very busy worrying about my morals and would sometimes stop a book that they thought would pollute Canada. In the early 1970's I ordered a book called *The Divine Mistress.* It was stopped at the border and I received a very severe letter informing me that is was only permissible for religious or educational books to enter Canada. I wrote an equally stiff letter back saying the book was a biography of Emilie, Marquise du Châtelet, an exceptionally gifted mathematician who did the first translation into French of Isaac Newton's *Principia,* perhaps the most important book of science ever written and is the foundation of all of physics. I did not dwell on her being Voltaire's mistress. The book came through on the next post!

CHAPTER 6

One thing that has always impressed me is how well we are served by doctors in our small communities. My distinguished friend Dr. Park from Johns Hopkins University, who I mentioned earlier, was full of praise for them. I did not know Dr. MacLeod but he always got special commendation from Dr. Park for being an exemplary country practitioner. There were a number of reasons for his admiration and they occasionally consulted with one another. Sometime before we came Mrs. Park became very ill, and neither Dr. Park, nor his son who was also a physician, had a clue as to what was wrong. In desperation they asked Dr. MacLeod to come, and when he open the door to their cabin and entered, he said, "She has typhoid." Apparently patients with typhoid gave off a characteristic odor which he immediately recognized even before he got to the bedside. As Dr. Park admitted to me, wise country practitioners were the real doctors. Mrs. Park recovered.

Much later my Ruth came down with something that the local doctors could not diagnose. She was very ill in the hospital in Inverness for quite a few days; it was a very anxious time. I have always wondered if she had Legionnaire's disease; in any event some of the symptoms were similar, and what was so worrisome, it can be lethal. She did get better and came home to the Harbour, but was very weak for months. While in the hospital she was wretched with continuous vomiting. This bothered me especially and one day I met her doctor in the hallway and asked if she might be becoming dehydrated and should she be getting intravenous fluids. I was sure I would be berated for telling a doctor what to do, but he looked at me in a startled fashion and rushed off to set it up. My instant thought was what a wonderful doctor: the needs of the patient came first; the doctor's dignity was nothing along side it. When she came home a most distinguished professor of medicine at Johns Hopkins, Dr. John Eager Howard, who came up each summer to visit his friend Dr. Park, came to call on us. I went to greet him as he got out of his car and said he had heard the Ruth had been very ill and asked what did she have? I said the doctors did not have a clue, and he replied that was clear evidence that there were good doctors in Inverness.

Those were the days of the old Inverness hospital. It was very small and somewhat rustic compared to the grand, modern-looking hospital that exists there today. Just inside the small entryway there was a bulletin board with the name and the room number of each patient. This was followed by RC or P; there were no Muslims, Jews, or Buddhists! Ruth had a small room, but just down the hall there was a larger room with a number of beds. This was for the infirm, very old ladies. Everyone's door was open, and suddenly in the middle of the night one of old ladies was shrieking and wailing—she had a nightmare. The nurse rushed down to her and began talking to her in a soothing voice to calm her down. After a bit it dawned on Ruth that she was crooning to her in Gaelic, and she said to me later, where, except in Cape Breton, would one have a wonderful nurse who could not only help palliate one ills but comfort one in Gaelic.

There are still those on the Island who speak Gaelic but the number is undoubtedly decreasing. When we first came it was rare, but occasionally one would hear it spoken. I was told that our neighbor Christie MacDonald (who was a Mackintosh) was a fluent speaker, but she would deny it, and refuse to tell me the Gaelic name of anything. She just shook her head and looked a bit annoyed; it was as though I was invading her privacy. What does remain, at least was common in the older generation when we first came, were accents in their spoken English from the old country. I remember talking to older Beatons in Broad Cove; they had that soft accent of the Western Isles.

To return to medical things, there is one big change: we now have a well organized system to take care of individuals that today are called "mentally impaired." For instance, school children with difficulties are cared for by the schools, and modern medical care including group therapy is there to help others. When I was in my teens in a small village in New Hampshire we had, what was then called a village idiot. Everybody loved him. If one met him on the street one yelled at him, "How's chicks" and he gave one the most engaging broad smile and say "How's chicks" right back, followed by a delighted laugh. Sometimes he got it in first, but it was the same. He was a ray of sunshine.

When we moved to Margaree Harbour there was Randy. He was a big young man, but always seemed harmless. He would come to the door to beg for cookies, but he was too persistent so eventually one had to discourage him. This turned out to be easy but we had to lie. He was terrified of dogs and we would tell him our dog was "cross" and he would be off. One day the wife of a couple who were friends ran into Randy and he said that he had met her father earlier. The "father" was her husband who she immediately teased him with what Randy had said. The next day Randy ran into the husband and said he had met his mother the day before. So the final score was even. Many communities had their Randy, but not any more. Randy did eventually go to an institution as did many others like him.

To outsiders like us, one of the biggest changes has to do with dentistry. When we came there were very few dentists, and there was so much evidence of bad teeth one assumed nobody ever went. Seeing people with decaying, or missing teeth was extremely common; that is no longer the case. Years ago a friend told us that she had a filling drop out and she went to a local dentist who put it back in and charged her a dollar. The shingle outside his office said dentistry and radio repair, and indeed there was someone in the waiting room with a radio in his lap. Things have changed.

Turning to religion and the care of the soul, it is my impression that when we first came there was far more tension between Catholics and Protestants than there is today. Our daughter Rebecca came up when we were still living at Fordview; she must have been 16 or 17. One of Rose Tompkins nieces took her to a young people's dance which she enjoyed very much. The only thing that bewildered her was that when the young man brought them home, he asked her if she would marry a Catholic. At that time there were barriers between the two religions, and the boy's question, which Rebecca took as a compliment, reflected that unease. As a distant, outside observer it seems to me that schism has almost, but perhaps not completely, disappeared today. This progress was partly the result of the efforts of Reverend Bellis of the Calvin United

Church and some of his counterparts among the Catholic clergy. This was brought home to me on a very special occasion of Dr. Bellis's retirement celebration.

We got to know Dr. Bellis because each summer he and his wife started a "Vacation Church School" in the basement in the church just across the street from us. They were both of them were wonderful teachers and the children were given lessons in practical handicraft, nature studies, a little religious instruction, and a big dose of music. Our Andrew, already at the age of 14 loved music and was clearly gifted at the keyboard, and Dr. Bellis was a tremendous fan of music, especially classical music. He and Andrew would have deep discussions as to whether Welsh hymns were superior to all others as Dr. Bellis maintained, or whether there were some other acceptable ones as well, which was Andrew's position. It was all very amicable and Andrew loved it all. He even played the organ once for a regular service. Both of the Bellises handled all human relations, with the young and the old, with grace and understanding.

Nothing made this point more clearly than the ceremony the whole community gave for his retirement after his many years of service. It was given in the school gymnasium in Margaree Center (then Cranton Section) and Ruth and I decided to go. We were delighted to see a huge crown, and the speeches were quite extraordinary. First there were touching testimonials and presents from his parishioners: they loved him. But then there were speeches by a Catholic women's organization (with a present), a remarkable speech by the young priest of St. Michaels Catholic church. His remarks were ones of warm praise, but his main message was that Dr. Bellis, more than anybody, had been responsible for the coming together of Catholics and Protestants at all levels. He preached harmony, mainly by example, and the valley had blessedly become a better place as a result of his ministrations and what he was as a person. It was a very moving evening. And for me it was clear evidence that relations had improved from when we first came.

I cannot finish discussing religion without mentioning Father Stanley MacDonald, one of the more splendid people in the area. He was, and is, admired by all, Protestants, Catholics, jews, and if there were any Muslims in the area, they certainly would be included. His manner, his wisdom, his compassion has been a benefit to us all. He called me up one day to ask me to join him to celebrate Father's Day at a local restaurant. We spent some time arguing who was the real father. I told him he won: his flock was far larger than mine.

I doubt very much that funerals have changed in any major way over the last fifty years, but they bring out the essence of the fine people of Cape Breton. I will begin with the funeral of Dr. Park, who however much respected and admired locally, was not a Cape Bretoner, but many of his local admirers were part of the funeral. He died at the age of 91 in his camp in 1969.

In those days Mr. Arthur Ingraham, whose house and store was up river up river from Margaree Center, was the undertaker. He in fact had three roles for in addition to undertaking, he also was the butcher and ran the ambulance. What seemed to me interesting, if not unique, he used the same station wagon for all three of his occupations. We all gathered in the United Church in Margaree Center and Dr. Bellis conducted the service, saying all the right nice things of Dr. Park. The coffin was in the main isle and Mr. Ingraham, wearing an appropriately dark suit and a very prominent pair of purple cotton gloves, sat in the front row. Each time we had to rise for a hymn or a prayer, he rose first, in front of us all, turned towards us, and with a grand, circular sweeping of his purple gloves would almost push us all to a standing position. And when the time came to sit down he gave us the reverse signal. Everyone knew exactly what to do. We pall bearers then carried the coffin down the street to the cemetery.

There are two other tales that occurred before the funeral. Old Mr. Ernest Hart, the maker of those wonderful chairs for which he was renowned, came to Dr. Park's son and said that since he and Dr. Park were both tall men of roughly the same size, he would like to donate the coffin he had built for himself. He explained that while he too was old, he had plenty of time to make another one for himself. The family was genuinely touched, but felt they could not accept such a kind and generous offer.

The other tale is that when Mr. Ingraham was putting the body in the coffin, he noticed with horror that the heart was still beating. No one had told the poor man that Dr. Park had a pacemaker.

To leap forward in years, Tommy Ben MacDonald's funeral took place in the United Church just across the road from our house. It was basically no different, although Dr. Bellis had retired and a newcomer ran the service. He had just arrived in the parish and he did a remarkable job of quickly learning all about Tommy Ben from the community and gave a moving eulogy. At that time the gifted and well known Cape Breton violinist Jerry Holland lived in Margaree Harbour and was a good friend of Tommy Ben and Christie. He played, with no accompaniment, the most beautiful piece and with such feeling that it had us all almost in tears. Somehow music can reach us in ways that words can never achieved. (He told me later the piece he played so wonderfully was *Hector the Hero*.)

CHAPTER 7

There have been big changes in the wildlife in Cape Breton since we first came. There are many species of birds that have dwindled or disappeared and some changes in the mammal population.

For instance there used to be kingbirds everywhere, but I have not seen one in some years. There are probably a few bobolinks still about but I have not seen one recently. They used to be everywhere: we even had a pair that nested in the hayfield outside our big window in Margaree Harbour. Swifts were abundant in earlier days; I have not seen one in ages. They used to nest in the chimney in our house in the Harbour. The chimney goes through the bathroom and while in the tub one could hear the young ones twittering away. This was true even when we had the old kitchen wood stove was lit. Its pipe came to the side of the chimney some distance above the bath; the adults would flutter down through the smoke to join their babies. (Jonathan actually watched this by holding a hand mirror in an old vent in the chimney in the cellar.) I used to wonder if they all suffered from respiratory diseases, and I kept asking myself when and how did they ever evolve such a peculiar behavior? Perhaps from swifts centuries back who nested in hollow tree trunks.

In general there seem to be fewer warblers too (although at this moment I see a yellow warbler in the hedge below my window). One suspects that all the migrating birds are faring less well in their winter habitats, along with the disappearance of the forests and the increase in humanity in their southern wintering grounds. I do not think it is due to anything that happened in Cape Breton.

There are many birds that are holding their own here. This is true for crows, robins and many other species. Bald eagles seem to be flourishing, no doubt helped by the universal banning of the insecticide DDT that affected the viability of their eggs. Most remarkable is the great numbers of humming birds that arrive in May. They are so small, yet they manage a marathon migration north and south every year. Perhaps so many of us putting out feeders for them has helped them flourish, not to mention all the flowers we plant nowadays.

The sea birds do not seem to have changed. On our coast, besides the gulls and the terns we have

black guillemots, an occasional loon, and sporadi-
cally gannets gracefully flying or diving for fish.
One spring I came in early in May and was driving
along the shore road to Inverness on a cold blustery
day when I noticed that there were thousands of
birds flying along the coast or resting in the water.
I pulled the car over and was thrilled to see they
were gannets, no doubt migrating to their nesting
grounds off the Gaspé. They certainly did not seem
to be on their way to extinction. We also saw quite
a gathering of them in the middle of the summer
on a whale watching expedition out of Bay St. Lawrence with my family; my granddaughter Ondine
is very keen on whales. There was a big school of
fish that were being pursued madly by a school
of graceful, leaping Atlantic white-sided dolphins
and an impressive array of gannets making their
spectacular dives in a feeding frenzy.

And in late summer one could occasionally find
modest flocks of whimbrels, a small curlew, arriving
from the distant arctic and feeding mostly on crow-
berry on bare hills near the sea. The mergansers
always fascinated me: I disapprove of the behavior
of the drakes. The elegant black and white males
join the females in the early spring, have their fun,
and then leave until the next spring. The abandoned
females make their nests along the Margaree river
and raise large broods that soon merge with other
broods to form congregations of 40 to 60 ducklings.
These crèches are supervised by only one mom,
but I assume the females take turns doing the child

care. This a fascinating bit of animal sociology: it is a mixture of child care cooperation by the females, and unspeakable selfishness, not to say boorishness, on the part of the males. Another memorable sight was when I was watching a bald eagle flying by our big window and being harassed by a herring gull. I was watching him with my binoculars when suddenly the gull came too close to his back, and with lightening speed the eagle flipped upside down, grabbed the gull in his talons, and calmly flew off to eat him.

As for mammals, long before we came there used to be caribou in the highlands, but they were hunted to oblivion. There was an attempt soon after we got here to reintroduce them, but the animals that were brought over did not survive. When we came we could still see caribou antlers attached above the doors of a few barns. There were some moose but the population was at a low ebb. Since then they have greatly multiplied, and a few are now being culled by hunters who have won a permit in an annual lottery. One evening we were having dinner at a friend's house in Belle Côte and from where I sat at the table I had a beautiful view straight up river. It was just at dusk and suddenly I saw what I thought was a horse on the road beside the river on the Belle Côte side. I looked up again a few minutes later and it was swimming across the river: my horse suddenly turned into a moose.

Another, relatively infrequent sight are mink. One summer there was a family at the Seal pool and it was delightful to see the young tumbling and wrestling at the water's edge. I have seen otters only once. I was fishing the top of the Tompkins pool early one morning before breakfast when we were at Fordview when two suddenly drifted by in the middle of the current of the river. They were not swimming but upright in the water, staring at me and barking. Clearly I was trespassing in their province.

I suspect that in the last 50 years in general there have been few other significant change in the mammal populations. The red squirrels, chipmunks, voles, foxes, deer seem always to be there. Once I was sitting on a boulder in a small brook in the middle of the woods on a warm summer day resting during a modest hike, and suddenly a tiny water shrew popped onto a rock right by me and briefly gave me the once over. It was an exciting moment for they are hard to find and rarely seen.

There certainly are annual fluctuations in the abundance of the various mammals, but after a lean year or two a species seems to thrive again. This is especially evident in the snowshoe rabbit (or hare). As I mentioned earlier, there were no coyotes when we came, but now they are everywhere. Those blessed with better hearing than myself often listen to their mournful chorus in the middle of the night. The only thing that has stopped their eastward invasion is the Atlantic ocean. Another mammal that has increased, or so it seems to the casual observer, are black bears. There are many more sightings in the more settled areas, and the Forestry people are very helpful and come with a huge trap on a truck, catch the bear, brand it with a generous streak of white paint, and cart it off to the distant highlands.

One does not have to be a biologist to find the wildlife and its changes fascinating.

Let me now turn to a subject close to my heart. It is something Ruth and I did almost every afternoon after my morning stint of writing. It is fishing.

When I first came to the Margaree I had only fished for trout, and in those days there were many brook trout in the Margaree. Inevitably one day a salmon took my fly, and again I came close to a heart attack. It was a small salmon, but it seemed enormous to me as it leapt out of the water right in front of me. After a spectacular fight, I finally beached it. It took quite some time for my heart rate to get back to normal.

I knew nothing about salmon fishing, but I learned from Jonathan, then still in his mid teens. He, being gregarious and curious, used to go down to the Forks pool, which was, and is, one of the most productive salmon pools. There were always a number of fishermen there, sitting on a log, waiting for their turn to go down the pool. One day Jonathan sat next to a tall, dignified elderly man and they soon started chatting. It was Dr. Park, and it was then that Jonathan began his lessons on salmon fishing. Every day when he came home, he would impart every detail he heard to me: that is how I learned about salmon fishing. The next year we were on the river and Jonathan introduced me to Dr. Park. From then on, along with Jonathan, I got my instructions directly from the master.

Jonathan talking to Dr. Park. My father is in the background wearing a cap.

In fact, we became fast friends, and both Jonathan and I learned more than fishing from him. One day Jonathan came home and described in considerable detail what had occurred at the Forks pool. While all the fishers sat on the log, a very aggressive newcomer just stood in one place, and fished over the hot spot without moving downstream after each cast. The other men on the log were furious and there was talk of going and pushing him into the river. Dr. Park got up slowly and said he would talk to the man. He first asked him if he could see what fly he was using. With considerable lack of grace he was shown it. Dr. Park looked at it and said he did not think that it was quite the thing, all the time pulling out his large fly box, crammed with flies he had tied. He reached in and said that, "You might have better luck with this, one, and here's another one that's good in this river." And after he gave him the forth one, he said in a gentle voice that it was the custom of the river to keep moving downstream after each cast." Profuse thanks, and the man began his steps downstream. It was not only a lesson for Jonathan, but for us all.

The rules were very different in those days than they are now. I think the limit was four fish could be taken in a day. Everyone carried a gaff to land the fish. All that has changed. Gaffs are no longer permitted, and all the big fish have to be returned; only the small grilse can be kept. This was largely the result of a decrease in the whole Atlantic salmon population, which fortunately is now to some degree stabilized. For the most part fishermen have accepted this change as a necessity, and everyone today gets the same enjoyment that they did years back. The other big change was that salmon nets in the ocean were forbidden, again as a conservation measure.

Ruth's first salmon was a memorable occasion. I have written it up previously in an autobiography (*Lives of a Biologist*) and will take the liberty of quoting myself:

As our youngest, Andrew, grew up enough to be left with his siblings, Ruth began to join me on the afternoon fishing expeditions. She soon developed into a first-rate fisher and cast an elegant fly. She concentrated on trout, which became her passion, but inevitably she hooked a salmon. It was a memorable occasion. We saw a fish stirring in the pool nearest our cabin and I urged Ruth to give it a try. She had hip boots on and could not wade out far enough to reach the fish, so we traded and she put on my high waders. She was lost inside them (and my feet were horribly compressed in her boots) but she cast out to the right spot and almost immediately was on to a big fish. She complained it was too big and wanted to give me the rod, but I urged her on and soon she was in the middle of a most dramatic struggle with a very active fish. Because she was very unsteady in the oversized waders I grabbed them from behind, and together we followed the fish. By that time my father, who was visiting, appeared, and he became as excited as the two of us. He kept calling encouraging things to Ruth with gentle advice, and then would roar at me things that always started, "For God's sake John...." get her to do this or that as though Ruth were not there. What I did not realize was that an entire road crew of men had left their machines to gather by the river's edge to watch the fun. After a great struggle the fish was finally landed, and at that moment a great cheer rose from the gallery on the bank. The fish weighed seventeen pounds and we have a group photograph with Ruth beside it where she and the fish look about the same size.

I should point out that the road crew was in the process of turning the dirt road into the blacktop that exists today. The year was 1962.

Part of the river lore are the guides and guardians who made it colorful. Let me begin with Ralph Watts who was the chief warden. He was a quiet and amiable man with a mission: to eliminate the poaching. This was a big problem before our arrival for numbers of men—a gang—would steal out at night and net a pool, or as Dr. Park told me he saw once, they would go out with torches and spear the fish. The fish were taken home where the women-folk would cook them and put them up in jars; as they would say, they were "canned." This was in an era when the economy was very low and stored food in preserve jars were a significant blessing.

I have been told that Ralph's approach was to pay a visit in the evening to the various well-know poachers and explain to them in a calm and considerate way that poaching had to stop and he was asking their cooperation. He made it clear to them the world was changing and they must be part of that change. It worked. Except for minor transgressions the old fashioned poaching not longer exists. I was also told that then Ralph, in his quiet way, made a brilliant move: he hired some of the most notorious poachers as river wardens, no doubt under the principle that it takes a thief to catch a thief. All has been mostly calm ever since.

There are, however, occasional blips. In recent years salmon conservation has produced a rule that all large fish (potential spawners) must be unhooked and immediately returned to the river after they have been reeled in. One day, a few years back, Tommy Murphy, a warden of great energy and good motives, came upon a small truck with two men taking down their rods. Tommy stopped and in the truck he saw a large salmon and immediately said it was much too big to take from the river. The men explained that the fish was essentially dead when they beached it and they did the only sensible thing and took it with them. Quick as a flash, Tommy seized the fish and ran with it down to the river where he revived it completely and it swam off. The men were not so lucky and lost their licenses and their rods.

Much earlier there were some colorful fishermen on the river. One we knew when we were still in Fordview. He was Monsieur Tabuteau, a distinguished Frenchman who was a world famous oboist who was with the Philadelphia Symphony. He was a rather gruff man in his fifties then, but we got along well with him and Madame. To give an example of his confrontational style, he told me once he hated music! He was full of river stories and there were stories about him. One day he was fishing down a pool and a well known bully would not move. When Tabuteau asked him to do so he got a surly refusal. Tabuteau put down his rod, unsheathed his gaff and with an angry scowl went for him. It was a different method from Dr. Park's, but equally effective. Another time he had a fish on and the tip of his bamboo rod broke off, but was held to the line by the guides. So the small tip slid down the line right to the mouth of the great salmon. In describing it (and this must be said with a strong French accent) he said, "Every time it jumped it looked as though it were smoking a cigarette."

Then there was the guide Johnny Stevens White (who could cast equally effectively with either hand, like a switch hitter) and was full of fun and had the most delightful command of the English language. One day I passed him on the street after he had moved to new quarters and asked him how it was going. He said, in his faintly Irish accent, that everything was wonderful: he had bought a new mattress and "it was like sleeping on ether."

When not fishing, my other passion was hiking. There are so many places for walks all around us and the possibilities were all inviting. There is a walk up a treeless hill in Broad Cove and down to a small beach that we all loved. It was there in late summer that we would sometimes see whimbrels, those small curlews. And the little beach was bestrewn with the most beautiful quartz pebbles so varied in their color (some of which invariably ended up on our windowsills back home). Another favorite was walking up Mackintosh mountain; the wood road starts just opposite the Chimney Corner beach and follows up a lovely small brook. From the road one could see patches of the beautiful miniature twin flower, the same flower that entranced the great father of botany, Carl Linnaeus, when he explored his native Lapland in the eighteenth century. Some times a logging road would take me to some remote spot and I would see that enchanting bird that is very bold, yet eschews civilization, the Gray or Canada jay.

In the summer of 1968, when I was young and spry, Jonathan and I decided to make a back packing trip up, or rather down, the Margaree river. We borrowed two enormous and ancient wood-framed back packs from Dr. Park which he had used for similar expeditions in years gone by. Ruth drove us to Cheticamp and from there we bummed a ride on a cart behind a tractor up the mountain inland of Cheticamp. Then we just took off west hoping to connect with the very upper portion of the Margaree river. Soon the walking got very rough. We had to cross a flat that was covered with young spruces which was made especially difficult by the two poles at the back of each of our 19th century knapsacks; it was non-stop wrestling for the poles caught onto the branches of every tree we passed. I remember the flat vividly to this day because that lovely bird, a greater yellowlegs was perched on top of one of the spruces and repeatedly sang its arresting alarm call. Clearly we were in his territory and the message was "get out." We finally did get to the river which was not much more than a brook and from then on we needed no compass; we just walked downstream. It was the beginning of August and we were blessed with four sunny days. Our first landmark was the

Twin Pool where two branches of the upper Margaree meet. Dr. Park had told us that the next pool down (the Top Pool) held salmon, but clearly none were there. As we moved down the ever widening river we discovered we could not just go down one side, but with increasing frequency we had to cross the river. And further down river, more than once the water was up to our waist. We lived in wet blue genes and boots but that was accepted without any notice. What was noticed was the incredible number of black flies, but we soon found that if we kept moving they did not bother us that much. For food we subsisted mainly on small trout that were everywhere and leapt at our flies eagerly. The gorges, such as the one at McCoy's pool were spectacular, but nowhere did we see a salmon: they had not come up river yet.

The McCoy pool way up the Margaree river.

In the afternoon of the fourth day we finally reached the Big Intervale, and Ruth was there, bless her, waiting for us in the car. On the way down to the Harbour she complained that never in her life has she encountered two such smelly people and made us open all the windows of the car. It was a great moment for each of us in turn to stretch out in the bath tub: bliss.

Best of all were the wonderful walks in the Cape Breton Highlands National Park. There the trails are kept up by the Park rangers with little bridges across the brooks. Some are modest walks, often up to a waterfall: perfect for a family outing.

My favorite was the Acadian Trail which I first encountered one afternoon. It was a time when Ruth was not well and a nurse stayed with her for four hours every afternoon which gave me time for an outing. I wanted to try for at least the beginning of the Acadian Trail for I knew I was limited in time. It starts at the Park information center and makes a 6 mile loop. My small terrier and I took the right handed beginning along a good size stream (to do the trail counter clockwise). Soon the path became more and more magical through the dense wood and along the stream where all the boulders were covered with moss. It was a fairy land. I looked at my watch and decided if I walked fast enough I could do the loop; it was so lovely I wanted to do it all. So at breakneck speed I followed the path up the brook and then up the side of a steep hill at the top of which I burst out on the most incredible view way up above the farms below and the ocean going off into the distance. It took my breath away. Then we barreled down hill back to the car and made it back home in time. The guide book says it takes three and a half to four hours: we did it in two, but I have done it many times since a normal speed and always felt a thrill, but nothing quite matched that first time.

As I look back at what I have written I feel as there is so much more to say, but that risks being boring. I wanted to give the essence of what Cape Breton, and the Margaree river valley have meant to me and my family over the last fifty years.

With the exception of Dr. Park, I have not said anything about the other summer people like ourselves who were our friends, and some of them our neighbors. I have done this on purpose because I wanted Cape Bretoners to take center stage: this is a book about them, for them, and in celebration of them. Those summer friends came both from the United States and Canada. Some are academic people like myself—they too had the summers off. And some are artists of great distinction, some are authors of great renown, and others have no such labels, but are just plain splendid people. I believe they all will support my view that this should be a book for a people and a place we all love.

Manufactured by Amazon.ca
Acheson, AB

14860904R00066